creative happy work

Follow your heart to a thriving business, life and world

By Kat Byles

A blueprint for creating a business that makes your heart sing
Suzy Walker, Psychologies Magazine

Acclaim for
Creative Happy Work
and the True Business Model

"True Business is a blueprint for creating a business that makes your heart sing."

Suzy Walker, editor in chief, Psychologies Magazine

"Following in the footsteps of Feel the Fear and Do It Anyway, The Power of Now and How to Win Friends and Influence People, Creative Happy Work is the agenda for a whole new revolutionary heart-centred way of working, a guide to a healthy thriving business for a connected universe."

Lucy Cavendish, Daily Mail

"This is yoga for your business. My plan became the creative, energetic heart of my project. What emerged was surprising, energising, and far larger than I expected. This has given me the courage to do effortlessly what I previously believed would be challenging. I cannot recommend Kat more highly. She is world-class."

Simon Haas, yoga philosopher and author

"Of all the courses, retreats, interventions I've done over the past 25 years, this has been the most life-changing, life-affirming and life-enhancing."

Anne-Marie Hoyle, principal consultant, TXM Consult

"True Business is a gift. It aligned me to the wisdom and the simplicity of my heart which is now my business guide and part of my decision making."

Sarah Rose Bright, Intimacy and Sex Coach

"My business was drifting, without direction and then I found Kat and the True Business model. I connected directly with my heart and found the right path which came with huge growth and financial success."

Mrs MummyPenny, personal finance blogger

"Working with Kat burst through two years of frustration and perspiration in about an hour and a half! From then I had a clear vision and set to work."

Martin Saunders, marketing director, Good Energy

"I have been able to realise a dream into a reality. My products are now available in stores and have had magazine coverage."

Nina Hossain, founder, Bliss Organics

"You have helped so many people run energetically in the right direction instead of wrong ones! Saved many people many years of woe and supported many people into fulfilling their purpose."

Katie Sarra, founder, The Institute for Relational Harmony Studies

"Kat has created something truly game-changing with her True Business model: a way to finally unite the personal and professional so that every business decision feels perfectly aligned with the impact and life you want."

Rowena Roberts

"True Business guided me to discover what I truly want to do next with my career and life in the most amazing and unexpected way."

Deb Lace-Kelly

For you Kat,
may you drink your own medicine

"It is only with the heart that one can see rightly;
what is essential is invisible to the eye."

THE LITTLE PRINCE,
ANTOINE DE SAINT-EXUPÉRY

Contents

Foreword

Kat is a genius.

Creative Happy Work is a unique and simple way of getting past the hype and into the heart of what matters most. To you. And your business. Even when you can't yet put it into words.

I've spent tens of thousands of dollars on marketing courses, from all the big names, and it's not added up to a fraction of what Kat has led me to in a few simple sessions together with the True Business model she shares here with you.

Previously, I'd get really excited about a marketing idea, and then quickly lose energy, because the approach wasn't true to who I am. It felt exciting at first, but wasn't coming from the core of my being and was therefore not sustainable.

Kat guided me through a process which anyone with a body, mind and spirit can do because the visualizations are so natural. Bubbling up from the deepest part of me came my True Business communication strategy: My purpose. My audience. My message. My channel. My skilful inspired action to take.

Simple. Shining. Clear.

Easy, effortlessly, enjoyably Kat helped me integrate everything I've been working toward for the last quarter century in a simple, clear plan that made sense not only to my head, but to my heart. Aligning and integrating all parts of me and my work together into one whole, from the inside out. Allowing me to take skilful, inspired action with my hands.

Head. Heart. Hands. All parts of me moving forward together, with clear intention and purpose to create what I want from the inside out. This is truly the simplest, easiest, most effective way to do anything. I call it getting into the flow, staying in the flow, and living in the flow.

Kat's genius is applying flow to business.

Getting into the flow for business IS Creative Happy Work.

How do you know the difference between hype and heart? Most of us have been trained out of listening to our heart. What I've noticed is this... when I feel the excitement of an adrenaline rush, it's hype. When I feel the deep peace and contentment of what's true for me, it's heart. Hype is like sugar, it gives you an immediate high, but drops you ten times lower than where you started. Heart is like a green smoothie, packed with goodness that nourishes every cell in your body for the long-term.

I'm astonished by the simplicity and effectiveness of the True Business model, of tapping into your heart to guide you toward creating and communicating the business of your dreams.

If you want to run your True Business, your Creative Happy Work, read on.

Thank you, Kat.

With gratitude,

LISA MK LING
Founder, Universal Dynamic FLoW
Author of *'DragonFly'* and *'Love Tank Parenting'*.
udflow.com

INTRODUCTION

"Change will not come if we wait for some other person or if we wait for some other time. We are the ones we've been waiting for. We are the change that we seek."
- Barack Obama

I wrote this book because I needed to find a way of being in business that heals rather than harms. A way of being in business that regenerates rather than depletes, that co-creates rather than competes. I needed inspirational clarity for a new chapter of my business created in harmony with the earth, my true nature and universal flow.

Creative Happy Work brought all of this to me and more besides. My hope is that this book brings this to you too. That it unleashes the creativity and business held deep within your Heart, a win-win for all.

We know that business as usual is making us sick. The relentless pursuit of growth and profit at all costs disconnects us from our true nature, from Mother Nature and Source, universal energy leaving us burnt out, stressed and anxious. The earth too.

The constant push for more – the myth that success is bigger, faster, stronger – is exhausting. Greed, corruption, environmental destruction brushed off as 'just business' physically hurts. Marketing manipulation pushing pain points, influencers pouting and flexing on social media is mind numbing. Even business with a purpose personally left me burnt out, nothing left to give. What then?

What if you don't want or value the Lambo? What if you want and value a calm, happy, peaceful life. A pristine untouched beach. A virgin forest teeming with life. A natural world revered, honoured and respected. Thriving biodiversity, rich soil. Abundant oceans, rivers and seas. Freedom of creative expression. Wellness and vitality. Making a contribution to a wider community you love being part of. Fulfilling your purpose and leaving a legacy. Yes please!

How do you fit into a traditional business system that doesn't value, respect or care about this, about what matters most to you?

You don't. You find another way.

"Follow your Heart" was whispered to me from deep within. Your wise inner compass, your heart, is the birthplace of your true nature and purpose; the gateway to Source, universal energy; a portal to connection, compassion and wisdom.

Follow your heart with inspired skilful action and you open up to a whole new world, to a thriving business and life that didn't exist before. What was once previously challenging becomes inevitable.

The True Business model shared in this book begins with connection to your heart. By connecting to and receiving your heart's wisdom you will align with your true nature and purpose, audience, message, offering and financial intention and structure that meets your needs for prosperity.

You receive crystal clear clarity, beyond doubt, so that action becomes skilful, a delight to take, an offering of love, devotional.

You learn to listen to and make wise decisions from your heart producing win-win outcomes. You experience a fresh new wave of creative emergence that is grounded and embodied moving through you and your business.

You see and understand with a compassionate lens the scripts, limitations and patterns you courageously and gently transcend without judgement, blame, bitterness or need for revenge.

Your mental health improves as you listen deeply to your feelings and needs and meet those needs. Your relationships become more wholesome meeting others as equals, co-creators and collaborators.

You learn to let go of the traditional push, chase and make it happen mode of business and step into a listen, receive and allow way of being in business.

You are being with and creating in harmony with universal flow, the highest form of creative intelligence that forms worlds.

Burnt out as a global communications director working with the biggest names in sport my heart led me to Antigua, an island in the

Caribbean. Here I walked barefoot on the sand, floated in crystal clear turquoise waters and ate coconuts and mangoes from the trees. Nature, the Caribbean Sea brought me back to life and restored my wellness. Then it began to feed me with inspiration for True Business.

Following my heart transformed ALL areas of my life, not just work. My partner, home, health, family relationships slowly rearranged into alignment with my true nature and purpose, bringing a deep sense of peace and harmony.

Then the Covid pandemic hit and the travel-related aspect of my business ended. This collided with the menopause and a deep inner change. It felt as if everything that had been so beautifully created was falling apart so I returned to my heart.

Listening, aligning with my true nature and purpose, a new vision began emerging. A deep calling to the ocean, a desire to co-create with ocean leaders and contribute to clean, healthy, abundant water, oceans, rivers and seas in our lifetime. Your heart will always light new pathways, even in the darkest moments.

This book and True Business model will connect you to your heart's wisdom and creativity, to who you are and what you are here for now. It will open you to fresh, inspirational clarity and a pathway in harmony with your true nature, Mother Nature and universal flow. A pathway to unfold your deep soul calling into successful creative, happy work and all the healing, wellness and fulfilment that brings.

What this book is not is a get rich quick scheme. It is not seven-days to a six, seven or eight figure business. Nor is it a book about how to write a 90 page business plan with sales and cash flow forecasting, profit and loss accounting, governance and tax returns. Creative Happy Work is dedicated to your lifeforce, to unleashing the divine creative energy within you to pour into your business, life and world.

If you are a YES to that, dive in.

In this book I'll share the True Business model, that was first shown to me in the divine morning light when immersed in the Caribbean Sea. Then you will play with it to discover your True Business, the Creative Happy Work ready to spill forth from within. This is a business, life and world that will make your heart sing.

CHAPTER 1

BRINGING YOU BACK TO LIFE

"Turn your Creative Spirit into an economic force for good."
- Prince.

It hasn't rained for three months and the hill in the village in Antigua is tinderbox brown. The hot sun has scorched the earth. The plants and trees are dying. Life is receding.

Finally come the rains. I close my eyes and breath in the sweet, sweet smell of water seeping deep down into the soil. The trees and plants draw the water in, and within hours it seems, shoot fresh new leaves. Lush green grass creeps back over the yard. The whole hill springs back to life, spilling forth a lively green. Life is bursting forth.

This is what it is like when you unleash your heart's wisdom and creativity on your business. After a period of stress, pushing, hard work, blood, sweat and tears, your heart opens and fresh inspiration, vitality and wellness flood in, bringing you back to life. A whole new world of opportunity that wasn't there before arrives like the rain. There is connection, happiness, wellness. Your True Business springs to life, making your heart sing. Your True Business supports happy, healthy abundant life on earth.

Business Leading with Profit Hurts

Traditional Business is hurtling in the wrong direction. We know this. Leading with profit, chasing the money at all costs, separates us from our true nature, from Mother Nature, from the creative stream of life. This hurts us and the earth.

It hurts when US politicians put gun sales and NRA pay-outs before the lives of children massacred in schools. It hurts when water companies continue to pollute the UK's rivers and seas with sewage, poisoning us, killing wildlife, making people sick. It hurts when developers destroy a pristine beach for another five star hotel.

It hurts when your soul slowly dies in a job you hate to pay the mortgage and feed your family. It hurts chasing money, sales and financial targets until you lose sight of why you went into business overwhelmed by stress, anxiety and burnout, fears of failure, or paralysed by perfection, your spirit and creativity dead inside.

Making business decisions leading with profit often causes catastrophe, Deep Water Horizon being one well-documented example.

The oil and petroleum company, BP, had received numerous health and safety warnings that a well, 41 miles off the south-east coast of Louisiana, USA, was unfit to pump oil. Behind schedule and over budget, the pressure for financial return led to people in the company ignoring these warnings. They pushed ahead.

On 20 April 2010 the oil well exploded, killing 11 people, injuring 17 others and spilling approximately 200 million gallons of crude oil into the Gulf of Mexico over 87 days. Wildlife devastated. Over 1,300 miles of coastline was affected in Texas, Louisiana, Mississippi, Alabama and Florida. BP estimated the disaster cost the business $61.6 billion. This omits the emotional cost of the lives lost, devastation to the families of those killed and injured; the costs to the health of people, wildlife and earth damaged by the pollution; the toxicity seeping into the earth's ecosystem.

Chasing profits, ambition, financial targets, promotions, recognition and goals, we fight against our nature, Mother Nature, universal flow and crash and burn.

This is where I found myself as a global changemaker and communication director working with the biggest names in sport to beat homelessness, burnt out, nothing left to give, at just 42. Our small, under-resourced team with a giant global vision, playing well beyond our means, was constantly struggling to stay afloat. Chasing bigger and bigger impact numbers with unstable financial foundations was energetically unsustainable.

A 90-hour working week was the norm, as was jumping on a plane or two to all five continents of the globe. Relationships with my family and friends became so depleted as to be non-existent, catching up on the phone while queuing to pay for my shopping. With no space for a life partnership, any attempts at relationships were dysfunctional at best. I felt painfully alone.

Under high stress, my leadership style became dictatorial, intimidating and controlling, or it was simply 'quicker to do it myself'. The addiction to over-working and achieving left me empty and time away from work was spent walking around a local lake in tears. Spiritually, mentally, and physically I was dying. It had to change.

Too many creative, sensitive, caring people tell me that they "can't do or aren't good at business." What they mostly mean is they don't want to sacrifice their health, relationships, creative freedom, natural beauty, the environment, hurt other people and the planet for money. They aren't turned on by the sport of profit making. They care deeply. They just don't know another way. Yet.

The Path of your Heart

"Follow your Heart," whispered my intuition. Stuck in burn-out, what did I have to lose?

Traditional business orientates from the head and gut. The heart is dismissed as airy-fairy, woo-woo, over emotional, misguided, fluffy, dangerous, weak. When I first heard these words – follow your heart - this was my first response. "That's a cliché, a bumper sticker, Steve Jobs has that covered. People will think you are crazy! Business leaders aren't going to listen to their hearts. The heart isn't businessy! What nonsense is this!" I initially rejected my heart's wisdom and intuition.

My experience has been quite the opposite. The heart is a powerful tool for transformation and change, it is our wise inner compass. The heart knows who we are and what we are here for. The heart transcends ego and separation, bringing connection, inspiration, vitality. With heart we create real, intimate and deep relationships that have respect, resilience, longevity and strength.

Our heart's wisdom is a gateway to inspiration, to Source, universal energy, the highest form of creative intelligence in the universe. Universal energy flows through the oceans, rivers and seas, through the moon and stars, through the plants, flowers trees and flowers, through you and me. It delights in creating. Let it delight in creating you and your True Business.

When we take consistent action inspired by our heart's wisdom, we build structures that nourish and support us, humanity, and nature to thrive. We direct resources, time, money, energy and attention towards what matters most, reducing waste. We create win-win outcomes.

Entrepreneur, Steve Jobs, was speaking from his wise creative heart in his 2005 Stanford University Commencement address when he implored us to: 'Have the courage to follow your heart and intuition. They somehow already know what you truly want to become. Everything else is secondary.'

Burnt out, ashamed and afraid I'd never recover and feel happy again, I followed my heart to Antigua, an island in the Caribbean for a holiday. Or so I thought. Swimming in the sea on the last day, my heart spoke loud and clear: 'You are not done. You need to come back and float in this sea every day for a month.'

An inner battle ensued – should I listen and go, or stay and get on with it! - and I fell out with my family for 'behaving like an irresponsible teenager'. Returning five weeks later, I walked barefoot on the sand, ate mangoes from the tree, watched the sun rise and set, and floated in the sea every day for a month. This immersion in nature finally restored my wellness. Then it began to feed me with inspiration for True Business.

Step by step, a business structure emerged that replaced the 90-hour week with a three-day week for the same level of income. This gave me time to be with and rebuild relationships with my family and friends and create a new life partnership. My home moved from living alone in Bath in the UK to Antigua living with my partner in a small village on the beach where I could swim in the sea and connect with divine inspiration every day. An abandoned puppy moved in, Scratch, bringing with him a heap of unconditional love; we planted bananas, papaya, coconuts and mangoes to grow abundantly in the yard.

We all have a True Business, so natural it doesn't feel like work. Whether it's an innate ability to teach, heal, inspire or transform. Perhaps it's to trade, create, write, paint, nurture, invent, pioneer new understanding, cook, code or grow herbs.

Working in harmony with your true nature, no longer fighting against it, you experience connection, creativity and wellness. Frustration, anxiety and overwhelm fall away to be replaced by clarity, peacefulness and fulfilment. There is a calm, inner confidence knowing who you are and doing what you came for.

A whole world of inspiration and possibility opens up before you that simply wasn't there before.

As you follow your heart, you will also experience that other elements of your life align and gently transform. You may move to a new home, a new country, or deepen your appreciation of the one you currently live in. Your life partnership may deepen or end and a new one begins that serves your true purpose. Your relationship with nature changes to reverence, appreciation and respect. You connect with more people who share your vision and values and a community begins to emerge. You are happy, healthy, and abundant.

Bex Shindler, founder, The Mindful Kitchen, is a plant-based chef on a mission to share earth-friendly high vibe food. She believes the food choices we make can be empowering for our own health and the planet.

Bex was fearful of stepping into business. Terrified of failing, paralysed by perfection, she was stuck watching others do what she was born to do, slowly dying inside.

Connecting with her heart, Bex began to align with her true purpose, message and channel to show up and add value to her audience. This deep and true inner alignment gave her the courage and inspiration to show up weekly on Facebook Live teaching simple plant-based recipes for our daily lives. By taking a stand for plant-based food that she loved, taking action led by her heart, her confidence began to grow.

Bex later shared a diary entry with me where she describes her experience of PR with Heart, and with her permission I'd love to share it with you too because it so beautifully describes the experience of following your heart's wisdom and creating in harmony with Source, universal energy.

> 'I feel so grateful for exactly where I am. For creating the path of my dreams, the life I want, for being in flow and aligned with my heart's true purpose. This has given me the springboard and motivation for the next phase of The Mindful Kitchen, and I am EXCITED! I can feel the life force running through my veins. So connected with Source and at peace. I feel I have everything I need in this moment.'

Only six months later, Bex became the plant-based chef for The Black Eyed Peas during their two-week song-writing retreat. They wrote a letter thanking her for creating food that tasted amazing and was incredibly nutritious; and for her passion and care, which had helped their creativity flow during long studio hours.

Bex also enjoyed a sold out season making plant-based food for retreats in Ibiza; created a plant-based recipe e-book and hosted a 21-day plant-based food challenge for 30 people, introducing plant-based food into their daily lives. She also moved from a big city to a village more closely connected to nature with a creative community.

There are so many more inspirational stories of creative leaders unleashing their heart's wisdom to create their True Business to share with you. I'd love you and your True Business to be an inspiration to creative leaders of the future, too.

Three Steps to Your True Business

There are three steps to your True Business, a simple framework to play with throughout this book, that lead you into a happy, healthy abundant life on earth. They are Connection – Alignment – Action.

Fig 1: True Business Model

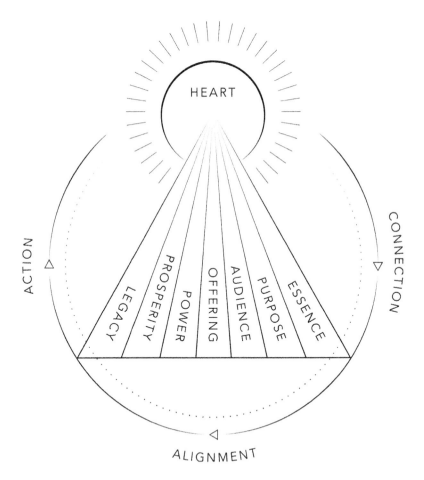

Step 1. Connection

Begin by connecting with your heart's wisdom and learn to listen, trust, and follow your heart's inner guidance. You can do this with a five minute meditation, by being outdoors with nature – swim in the ocean, walk in the forest. Take out your journal and write, draw or paint. Use dance, breathwork, playing with your children or pets.

There are so many ways to shift from your mind into your heart. We will explore this more in the coming chapter with an invitation to get curious, experiment and find your preferred ways to build your connection, trust, and relationship with your heart.

Step 2. Alignment

With a clear connection to your heart, you can now listen and receive alignment with your unique True Business blueprint:

Essence, your inner being, true nature in a relaxed state

Purpose, why you are here on earth, in business, what you are here to do

Audience, who your essence and purpose naturally serve to thrive

Offering, what you provide to serve your audience in return for payment

Power, the deeper truth of you as a powerful creator, resourceful adult

Prosperity, all your needs naturally met in harmony with creative abundance

Legacy, your lasting impact and contribution to the wider world

Step 3. Action

With connection to your heart and alignment with your True Business blueprint, you open up a pathway that fulfils your true nature and purpose.

Here action is inspired and skilful, taken as an offering of love, free from attachment to a particular outcome. Action becomes an act of devotion. This is Karma Yoga.

On the path of your heart, action is now in harmony with your true nature, Mother Nature and Source, universal energy. It is towards the direction of your destiny, towards peace, prosperity and progress. What was once challenging becomes inevitable.

The Hallmarks of a True Business

As you follow the path of your heart, your True Self emerges and your business becomes an expression of your higher nature. My personal experience was that I also became more aware of and sensitive to lower nature impulses of greedy, corrupt, lazy, self-interested ego agendas, both my own and those expressed by others. Compassion, boundaries and guidance from my heart is essential, as is returning to these hallmarks of a True Business.

1. Lead with your Heart's Wisdom

Traditional business leads with profit. Your True Business leads with your heart, your wise inner compass and creative engine. The inspiration, intuition and intelligence of your heart opens you to a whole new world of opportunity previously inaccessible operating solely from your head and gut.

2. Create in harmony with Source, Universal Energy

We are all creative beings. We are part of an expression of Source, universal energy that delights in creating. Traditional business is separate from Source, most often oblivious to its existence. Your True Business creates in harmony with Source, your business becomes the vehicle for the creative expression of pure Source inspiration.

US author, Michael Singer, illustrates this perfectly in his book *'The Surrender Experiment: My Journey into Life's Perfection'*. As a young man, Michael becomes conscious of the voice in his head and heads off to a woodland in Florida to meditate. Life has other plans. People keep showing up!

One day a woman arrives, pitches a tent and joins him in meditation. Then he returns home to find her building a house on his land. His initial response is along the lines of: "What a cheek! What person in their right mind builds a house on someone else's land without even asking?" He leaves to meditate and afterwards returns to help her build it.

The house becomes the heart of Temple of the Universe, a yoga and meditation centre for inner peace. Visited by well-known spiritual teachers, it has welcomed hundreds of thousands of people from all around the world and has since grown to encompass 600 acres of woodland. The house was so beautifully built that other people asked if they'd build them a house too, inspiring a homebuilding business, Built to Last.

Michael's logical mind would have shut down this creative emergence when the woman arrived with her tent. He chose instead to create in harmony with the flow of life. It didn't stop there. He built a billion dollar medical database company with the same approach.

3. Fulfil your True Nature and Purpose

Fulfilment of your purpose, your soul's calling, is your focus for your True Business, not shareholder returns, as in a traditional business.

US actress and film maker Reese Witherspoon's purpose is to share women's stories on the big screen and change the women's narrative in US culture. She founded Hello Sunshine to share stories written by women, with a female lead, brought to the big screen by women.

Reese pitched her business to investors and was told no one would want to watch films with a female lead: it would not be profitable. So she invested her own money, which, she was also told, was a mistake.

Reese Witherspoon's first two films, 'Wild' and 'Gone Girl', grossed half a billion dollars. She has produced the successful TV series 'Big Little Lies', 'The Morning Show' and 'Little Fires Everywhere', written by women, staring women as the lead. Her true nature and purpose is the focus for her True Business and she is wildly successful, inspirational and profitable.

Business with a purpose beyond profit is proven to be more profitable. US consultants Collins and Porras in their book *'Built to*

Last' (1992) showed that companies guided by a purpose beyond profit returned six times more financial returns to shareholders than purely profit-driven rivals.

4. Balance Being and Doing

Traditional business is action orientated, weighted towards goals, to-do lists, hard work making it happen. We get caught in day-to-day tasks, wear busy as a badge of honour, run around chasing our tails. Rest is time wasting and lazy. It is not billable hours! This is counter-productive, causing stress and burn out.

Your True Business begins with being, making space and quiet to listen to your heart, the wellspring of ideas, inspiration and Creative Flow. Here action is smart and skilful in the direction of your destiny. There is a healthy a balance of being and doing, feminine and masculine, Ying and Yang.

Running Authentic PR, there were times business dried up. I'd knock on doors, bash out 20 emails, hustle for business. The times I stepped away from the computer, went for a walk in the woods, focused on simply being, an inspired idea or client always arrived at my door.

5. Being of Service

True Business exists to be of service while traditional business pushes sales and financial targets.

The pressure of sales and financial targets disconnect us from our true nature and being of service, pushing business in an unhealthy direction. Employees of US bank, Wells Fargo, under intense pressure to reach sales targets created millions of fake customer accounts falsely inflating the business. The bank was ordered to pay a $185 million fine and 5,000 employees were fired.

Launching PR with Heart, an online course to share your message, inspire your audience and grow your impact, I set myself a small sales target of 20 people from my existing network. This created a pressure that shut down my connection to Source. I turned to the prayer from Course in Miracles, a spiritual thought system written in 1975, championed by Marianne Williamson in The Return to Love:

> 'Dear God, where would you have me go?
> What would you have me do?
> What would you have me say?
> And to whom?'

With this focus on service conversations opened up, introductions and referrals were made. Listening deeply to potential participants, I shared valuable insight and professional experience freely to move them forwards. Creative leaders ready to grow their audience and impact joined the course. No email blasts. No pushing pain points and presenting myself as the one and only solution. No sales funnels, countdown clocks, long sales pages to scroll through with bonuses nobody wants. Simply showing up and focusing on service.

6. Respects and regenerates nature

True Business respects Mother Nature as a living, breathing ecosystem. Nature is sacred, to be deeply respected. Nature is our life force, health, wellness and abundance. When we create in harmony with nature, we regenerate and eco-systems regenerate.

In traditional business, the natural world is an economic resource to be exploited and depleted for financial gain. This has had a disastrous impact. In just 50 years, half the earth's wilderness has been destroyed for commercial gain. The 2020 WWF Living Planet Report highlights a 68% decline in animal population, half of the earth's coral reefs are lost, a fifth of the Amazon Rainforest gone. Water companies pump sewage into rivers and seas; rainwater run-off from agriculture sends sediment, pesticides and faecal contamination into ditches, streams and rivers killing marine life and making humans sick. The World Health Organisation estimates that 1 in 8 deaths per year are due to air pollution.

The poor design of traditional business, greed and laziness (we can easily imagine so much better) is destroying the biosphere, destabilising our climate and killing us for money.

Clare Dubois, founder of Tree Sisters, a global network of women reforesting the earth, puts it simply: "We cannot have an economic system built on the death of nature. We have to re-imagine the economy."

Environmentalist Paul Hawken agrees and takes this a step further: "If we consider that global warming is happening for us—an atmospheric transformation that inspires us to change and reimagine everything we make and do—we begin to live in a different world. We see global warming as an invitation to build, innovate and effect change, a pathway that awakens creativity, compassion and genius."

In 1994, Ray Anderson, CEO Interface, a US-based industrial carpet company, chose this pathway and became a global pioneer for sustainability. After reading Paul Hawken's book The Ecology of Commerce: A Declaration of Sustainability, Ray became aware of the corporate machine plundering the earth and believed that one day this would be deemed criminal. Ray set about re-imagining Interface's business model to become sustainable by 2020.

This choice opened Interface to new product development, waste reduction and renewable energy. The company reduced greenhouse gas emissions by over 80%, saved $438 million in waste costs and reduced its fossil fuel consumption by 60 percent. It also doubled revenue to over $1 billion. Anderson opened the way for companies killing the earth for profit to reimagine their business and transform.

7. Create prosperity for all

One of the most common fears I hear about following your heart is that it won't pay the mortgage and feed the family. There is a globally shared false belief that we have to sacrifice ourselves and the environment to make money, a lose-lose.

My experience has been the opposite. As you pour your heart and inspiration into building your True Business, you build a structure that meets your needs to be healthy, happy AND prosperous as you contribute towards humanity thriving, a win-win. Your True Business is one way that you can follow your heart and be prosperous.

A Review - Traditional v True Business

What is your current business experience and what would you love it to be?

Scan the hallmarks and characteristics of a traditional and True Business in the table below. Take two coloured pencils and with the first circle the characteristics that represent your business experience now. With the second coloured pencil ring the characteristics you'd love to experience in business.

What do you notice? Perhaps striving for sales and growth has pulled you into the egoic approach of traditional business, or a period of reduced clients has triggered scarcity pushing you into panic, hustling, hard work, blood, sweat and tears? No judgement. Simply become aware what the contrast is highlighting for you.

Characteristics	Traditional Business	True Business
Intelligence	Head Logic + Gut Instinct	Heart Embodied Wisdom
Leads with	Profit	Source, Creative Energy
Fulfils	Shareholder Returns	True Nature and Purpose
Orientation	Doing	Being + Doing
Focus	Sales + Growth	Service + Value
Nature	Resource, Exploited	Life force, Sacred, Respected

Work Ethic	Blood, Sweat and Tears	Nourishment and Pleasure
Prosperity	Sacrificed for Profit	Generated for All
Energy	Force	Flow
Financial Belief	Scarcity	Abundance
Power	External, Acquisition	Inner, Wisdom
Legacy	Short-term interest	Lasting for generations
Leadership	Control and Command	Connect and Inspire
Style	Aggressive	Compassionate
Route to Success	Competition	Co-operation
Support	Lone warrior	Collaboration
Mental Health	Stress, Anxiety, Burn-out	Peaceful, Calm, Contentment

Journal

Journaling encourages connection with our heart's wisdom and inspiration. It can also clear away limitations, doubts and fears returning us to Creative Flow. Take 20 minutes or so to journal around these questions.

1. What does your True Business look and feel like to you?
2. What beliefs and behaviours have you let go of in your True Business?
3. What new beliefs and behaviours have you embraced in your True Business?
4. How often do you currently listen to your heart in business?
5. What becomes possible and opens up for you when you do?
6. What would you love your True Business to contribute to the world?
7. What is one skilful action to take towards discovering your True Business today?
8. What commitment are you making to yourself and your True Business?

You CAN have a business that makes your heart sing. A financially flourishing business that nourishes you on a deep soul level and sets your creative spirit free to make the contribution towards a fairer society for all. This is your destiny.

You don't need to know how. Simply be willing and open. Let's take the first step and connect with your Heart - the gateway to your wisdom, creativity, transformation. Let's open up a whole new pathway to a happier, healthier life, business and world. **_Your True Business supports happy, healthy abundant life on earth._**

CHAPTER 2

CONNECT WITH YOUR HEART

"The richness I achieve comes from nature, the source of my inspiration."
- Claude Monet

I t's early morning in our tiny Caribbean village by the sea in Antigua and the sun is rising over the hill, not another soul in sight. Stepping into the crystal-clear water, silky and cool on my skin, my body and mind gently awaken to the day. Swimming slowly away from the shore, I watch the sea floor deepen below me, noticing the wavy patterns on the seabed, enjoying warm, gentle sunshine on my face. There is nothing but peace and beauty. I breathe it in.

It is here, held by nature, the ocean, the morning light, that I clearly hear the wisdom of my heart. In nature's quiet stillness divine inspiration flows. Immersed in water, worries washed away, answers to questions are clearly heard. Decisions are cleanly made. Deep nourishment and confidence flows. Your heart is the gateway to wisdom and a whole new world.

Ways to Connect with your Heart

There are many ways to connect with your heart's wisdom; the gateway Source, Creative Flow and inspiration. Being in nature, meditation, yoga, painting, writing, dancing, sports, gardening, cooking, dancing, photography, running and playing in our imagination, to name a few. You will have your own preferred way of connecting to your heart's wisdom, creativity and all the healing and transformation this offers to you and your business.

It helps to turn down the noise from your mind and the external world, giving priority to space and quiet to hear your heart. Turn off media, social media, experts telling you to do it a certain way and tune into your heart's wisdom and transmission instead. Personally I also gave up caffeine because it amplified the volume and speed of my mind chatter to unmanageable levels.

Immerse in Nature

Being outdoors in nature is by far my preferred way to connect with my heart and Source, universal energy. There is a huge amount of scientific research demonstrating what we intuitively know to be true - nature reduces stress, anxiety and depression and inspires connection and creativity. Natural beauty, awe and wonder also inspires compassion, our higher nature, while improving our happiness, vitality, health and wellbeing.

Wallace J Nichols is a US marine biologist and author of *Blue Mind: The Surprising Science That Shows How Being Near, In, On, or Under Water Can Make You Happier, Healthier, More Connected, and Better at What You Do.*

Blue Mind is the calm, connected serenity we experience near water. This is in contrast to Red Mind, a state of anxiety and overstimulation from the speed of today's society, processing high amounts of information, making fast decisions. If we spend too much time in Red Mind, we end up burnt out with a feeling of detachment, dissatisfaction and lethargy: Grey Mind. Being by the water is the medicine we need to soothe and restore our Blue Mind.

Wallace explains that when we are by water, our brains have much less to process – just a single vision of the horizon, the gentle sound of waves on the shore. This gives our brains far more bandwidth for inspiration and ideas.

We hear stories of scientists and mathematicians working tirelessly on problems, only to find the solution comes to them when they take a break and go for a walk. Here, immersed in nature and moving the body, energy and inspiration flows.

Burnt out, over worked, his family in crisis, feeling as if he was failing as a father, South African filmmaker Craig Foster began to immerse himself in the wild, natural beauty of the sea with free-diving. On a dive, he encountered an octopus and this inspired him to pick up his camera again.

Craig went to the sea daily, chronicling the life and intelligence of the octopus and the relationship they formed. This inspired the magical film 'My Octopus Teacher', sharing beauty and wonder of the natural world with millions of people on Netflix.

The natural world opened Craig's heart, restored his wellness and began feeding him with inspiration, leading him and the team to create their life's work. My Octopus Teacher is a lasting legacy that continues to inspire millions of people to respect and connect with nature and the ocean more deeply. The film was recognised internationally with a BAFTA and an Oscar. Craig became the founder of The Sea Change Project - storytelling for ocean conservation.

Find the places in nature that open your heart and inspire you. Notice the sounds around you, both near and far away in the distance. Bring your awareness to the colours, plants and trees moving in the breeze. You might notice birds, animals, even insects. As you do, begin to become aware of the energy of life moving through nature surrounding you. Become aware that this energy is moving through you too. You are nature too and at one with this life energy, Source, streaming through you and the world around you. Here, you can hear your heart speak clearly and freely to you.

Meditation

The ancient practice of meditation allows us to connect deeply with the calm, sacred centre of our True Self. By focusing on our breath, a mantra, observing our thoughts and feelings, judgements and attachment, we can step beyond them and deepen our presence with our true nature, listen to the wisdom of our heart.

I'm reminded of the Rumi Poem:

> "Out beyond ideas of wrongdoing and right doing,
> there is a field. I'll meet you there."

This has been the gift of meditation to me, to step beyond my mind into my wise, sacred heart, my True Self.

Guided meditation is one of the main tools we will play with throughout this book, activating your imagination to receive your sacred heart's vision, wisdom and creative power. This is very different to visualising that car, house, relationship, or money you want. As you sink into your heart, your imagination begins to unfold before you, revealing your deepest desires, vision and love. You receive your imagination rather than directing it towards a particular outcome.

Scientific research shows that imagination shifts activity in the brain from the amygdala, the primal survival brain that processes fear and threat for a flight, fight or freeze response, into the frontal cortex, the creative brain, the hub of creativity, where new connections are made. Here we are open to our heart's wisdom and creative inspiration flows.

Journal

Journaling is in my personal top three of powerful practices for connection with your heart's wisdom, intuition and creative inspiration - you can write your heart's wisdom into being. Journaling can also help you become aware of, and clear limitations, doubts and fears returning back to the Creative Flow.

Julia Cameron's gift of a book, The Artists Way, a process for recovering your creativity and setting your creative spirit free, introduces us to Morning Pages, three pages or 20 minutes of writing a stream of consciousness first thing in the morning. By releasing the noise of your mind onto the page, you find you can go beyond it, connect with your heart and inspiration comes.

When I first discovered the morning pages in the mid 90s this free writing practice supported my recovery from an eating disorder as I wrote my way back to wellness. Ten years later, I revived the Morning Pages journaling practice and ended up writing articles for the UK's leading ethical and authentic lifestyle magazine, becoming acting publisher. Journaling daily opens up my connection to my heart allowing creativity to pour through me.

Yoga

Yoga is union with the divine. It offers us a way of being that unites us with our sacred heart, our true nature and purpose, with Source, creative consciousness. Asanas are the yoga postures that facilitate the union of our body, mind and spirit. By bringing yoga off the mat and into our business, we have a way of being in business that is in harmony with our true nature, nature and consciousness.

The Arts - Painting, Music, Dance

All arts - music, painting, photography, singing, chanting, writing - invite transcendence beyond our ego mind, into our heart, opening up to Source, creativity.

Psychotherapist, Intimacy Coach and Artist, Katie Sarra paints to connect to her heart. She paints the beauty of nature - the ocean, animals, birds, the starry night sky – expressing creative energy and life force on the canvas.

Working with Katie, I witnessed periods of her painting preceded big creative developmental leaps in her business and personal life. Moved by her connection to her heart, she pours the wealth of this creative energy into her therapy business, The Institue of Relational Harmony Studies. She developed the pioneering 'Body Poem' modality to access the aspects of ourselves we have abandoned and serve clients deeply with radical acceptance. Following her heart with courage and conviction, she sold her home in the UK and moved to an eco-community in the Portuguese mountains.

Prayer

Prayer has invited connection with our heart, with the Divine through the ages. Seek out or write the prayers that serve your personal connection.

Two simple lines from Tosha Silver's *'Full Abundance, Change Me'* prayer help me let go of any ego agendas, attempts to control outcomes and reconnect with the path of my heart with a sigh of relief:

> "Let everything that needs to go, go.
> Let everything that needs to come, come."

Movement

Walking, running, dancing, shaking, swimming, windsurfing, any physical sport moves us beyond the limitations of our thinking mind. Through movement, we come to embody the universal creative energy and be enlivened by it. This is especially important if you are a physical person not endeared to the idea of meditation or other stillness practices. Movement outdoors, in nature, even better.

American author Jean Huston tells the story of a tribe in West Africa who unite in dance to connect to their heart's wisdom, to Source. The village comes together to dance and sing solutions to an engineering problem with the village well into being.

Breathwork

Breathwork - breathing exercises and techniques focusing on your conscious awareness of your inhale and exhale - is a powerful tool to open your heart, connect to Source, creative inspiration.

Breathwork improves our emotional state, moving us through experiences of anxiety, stress, trauma, pain, grief and depression; enhancing connection, love and joy. It can move stagnant or blocked energy, which is causing us to feel low or stuck, opening us back up to our higher nature.

There are many different techniques available including Connected Breathwork, Shamanic Breathwork, Holotropic Breathwork, Vivation, Transformational Breath, Clarity Breathwork using techniques such as box breathing, alternate nostril breaths, pursed lip breathing, diaphragmatic breathing. To begin, you may like to work with a breathwork practitioner who can guide you in your breathwork practice with awareness of any health issues: there are many breathwork sessions freely available online for you to try it out.

You can combine breathwork with cold water therapy, immersing into an ice bath, using the Wim Hof method, which invites patience and commitment to master your body and mind and open up your connection to your true nature.

Divination Tools

Divination tools such as The I Ching, astrology, runes and tarot cards have served many over the ages to connect to natural creative cycles and rhythms. Explore, play and find the divination tools that resonate and support you.

The I Ching is a particular favourite discovered in my late teens. Drawing on Taoist philosophy, it supports you to live in harmony with the Creative to experience prosperity, understanding and peace of mind. You shake three coins. Heads equals three, tails equals two. Add up the value. Odd numbers form a broken line, even numbers a solid line. Shake six times to make six lines, known as a hexagram. There are 64 different hexagrams offering wise guidance to restore your humility and connection to the Creative Flow, returning you to your heart.

Gratitude and Appreciation

One of the simplest ways to connect to your heart is to focus on gratitude and appreciation. Appreciate the moment you are blessed to be living in; the miracle of your body; the relationships, family, loved ones you hold close to your heart; the environment you are currently in, the remarkable beauty of Earth, our blue planet.

Take a moment and bring your awareness to all that you appreciate. Journal about what you are grateful for, keep a gratitude journal for a month and notice how much more frequently you are connected to and creating in collaboration with your heart's wisdom and universal energy when you do.

These are a few of the many ways to connect with your heart and all the wisdom, creativity, inspiration and power for transformation your heart holds. You will have your own natural preference and may already be turning to this practice daily. If not, begin with nature - walk with all your senses, rather than walking through with your head down worrying about a problem or distracted by your phone, and listen.

Required Learning and Development

As you practice connecting with your heart, then comes the courage, growth and development required to lead with your heart's wisdom in business.

You learn to tune into, receive and hear your heart's wisdom and intuition beyond the doubts, fears; the voices of your parents, boss, experts, friends; the noise of the herd on social media, press; beyond education, social conditioning.

You learn to trust and act upon your heart's wisdom even when it appears counter intuitive, makes no logical sense or requires you to take big leaps of faith.

You learn to stand alone on the occasion your heart's wisdom says go right and everyone is going left yelling at you that right is dangerous, you are foolish, it is far better to go left.

You learn to be vulnerable, to freely and generously communicate your heart's wisdom to others without expectation, manipulation, coercion or attachment to a particular outcome. To give space to others to follow the path of their heart too, even when it takes you in different directions.

You learn to have compassion for yourself when you experience resistance, find yourself caught in the same old pattern, frustrated you aren't making progress, nothing is working, you can't bring your vision into being no matter what you do.

You learn to soothe, listen to your feelings, meet your needs with gentleness and kindness, which you will notice begins to regulate your nervous system.

You begin to let go of the pattern of hard work, forcing and grasping and surrender to the Creative Flow and remain present to life's invitation and in congruence with your heart's vision of your True Business. It takes practice and devotion.

What if leaders at BP at Deep Horizon had taken a moment to listen and led with their heart's wisdom rather than given in to the pressure of profit? As well as the lives, wildlife and financial saving, what creative solutions, innovations, discoveries and progress would have been made? What valuable business evolution for BP, humanity and the earth would have emerged?

Where would the world be now if Exxon Mobil executives had led with their heart's wisdom and shared scientific research into the greenhouse effect of burning fossil fuels conducted in 1981? What innovation, technology, reality would have emerged? Instead, led by profit, millions of dollars were spent lobbying press and politicians to seed doubt and confusion, stalling and preventing action as they continued to pollute and poison.

50 years on Planet Earth is suffering the environmental crisis the scientific research predicted with millions of lives, homes, businesses and species lost. 50 years wasted in the wrong direction. 50 years of lost creative innovation. By listening to wisdom we could have been adapting and living in harmony with the earth.

Guided Meditation

Your Heart's Vision of your True Business

This is a guided meditation to explore your experience of business leading with your heart to contrast with your experience of business leading with profit and the egoic mind.

If you prefer to listen you can download and listen to the guided meditations featured in this book at katbyles.com.

Guided meditation is an invitation to connect to your heart by playing in your imagination. There is no right way. All of us experience our imagination differently. You may receive visuals, sensations, sounds, symbols, colours or emotions. Your experience may be clear and direct audio. It may be unexpected, surprising. It may not make sense until later. You may not experience anything at all and wake up the next morning with an inspirational download or it all becomes clear in the shower.

Bring an open mind and heart, a playful sense of curiosity, and you are good to go. If you find yourself shutting down, resisting, controlling the outcome, return to a playful sense of curiosity - 'I wonder...?'

You may also like to clear your mind with a lovely walk in the fresh air, move your body to a piece of music you love, have a good shake, yoga or a HIIT work out. You can also just dive in! I love connecting to my heart where ever I am - on a busy train, waiting for a friend to join me for coffee. It's always there.

When you're ready, turn off any distractions. Get comfortable and gently close your eyes. Take a breath deep into your belly and bring your awareness to your thoughts and feelings, be the compassionate observer, no judgement, simply notice what is going on for you in this moment.

Bring your awareness to your body, noticing sensations in your body. Relax your head, your throat and neck. Drop your shoulders. Invite relaxation into your arms, hands and fingers. Invite relaxation into your torso, your spine and lower back. Let your belly out. Feel your sitting bones making contact with the chair. Relax your legs, knees, ankles, feet and toes. Breath loving kindness into the whole of your body, every single cell.

Next, step into innocence, the bridge into your heart, where you can listen to your heart's wisdom and come into harmony with

Source, the energy of life itself and what it wants to create with you now in your True Business.

Let your imagination take you into nature, a place that you love. Feel your feet on the earth, warm sunshine on your face, a gentle breeze on your skin. Take in the beauty around you, breathe in and smell the freshness of the earth. Your body relaxes even more. Life has your back and is always serving your highest flourishing.

Choose to receive the wisdom of your heart. In your imagination, draw a golden circle on the earth in front of you. This represents the end result for you in business leading with your heart, your True Business.

Step into the golden circle and receive the essence and vision of your heart leading in business. Breathe it in, give yourself space and time for your experience to emerge more brightly.

Notice who you are being. What impact does your heart leading have on you, on your audience, on the world? What word describes the vibration of your business leading with heart, your True Business.

Step back into nature, your feet on the earth, beauty and wonder all around you. You can see the golden circle of the end result in business leading with your heart. Next to it draw a second golden circle. This is the end result for you in business leading with profit, leading with your egoic mind, your traditional business.

Step in and receive your traditional business. Notice who you are being here. What impact does this traditional business create for you, your audience, the world? What word describes the vibration of your business leading with profit and egoic mind?

Step back into nature, your feet on the earth, breathe in the beauty and wonder all around you. You can see both the golden circle of business leading with your heart's wisdom, your True Business and the golden circle of business leading with profit, your egoic mind. Notice the contrast. Which are you most familiar with? Which is most attractive to you? Which do you choose?

The invitation is to step back into the business leading with your heart, your True Business. Immerse fully back into the vibration, the impact your heart creates for you, your audience and world.

Once you are fully immersed ask what is the potent daily practice to connect with your heart's wisdom? Make a commitment to you, your audience, the world to immerse yourself in this daily and receive your heart's wisdom.

Take a deep breath and when you are ready, gently come back. Pick up your pen and paper and journal around your experience to continue to flood you with insight and inspiration into your business leading with heart and business leading with profit.

Journal

If you'd like to journal and explore your connection with your heart a little more, pick up your pen and write for 20 minutes around these questions.

1. What is your current relationship with your heart's wisdom in business?
2. How would you love your relationship with your heart to be in business?
3. What daily practice will you introduce to connect with your heart's wisdom?
4. What fears cause you to block, doubt or ignore your heart's wisdom?
5. What does ignoring your heart create for you, your audience, the world?
6. Who are the people leading with heart in business that you respect?
7. What qualities and behaviours do they inspire in you?
8. What is it about following your heart in business that calls you forward?

We've explored the ground-breaking True Business model, how it works, how it radically differs from traditional business. The pursuit of profit at all costs now replaced by leading with your heart's wisdom and the radically different outcome this creates.

On connecting with your heart, the next step is to align with your True Business blueprint, beginning with your true nature and purpose, who you are and what you were born for. Let's receive that now and drink it in.

CHAPTER 3

ALIGN WITH YOUR TRUE NATURE AND PURPOSE

'When I became open in who I was, I found my purpose there.'
- Jill Ellis, former coach of USA Women's Soccer Team

The Latin name for the banana tree is *Musa acuminata*. We've planted banana trees in the yard. A tiny orchard of banana, papaya, mango, local lemon, coconut and moringa trees are emerging. I'm mesmerised.

The banana tree trunk is made up of its leaves, which are huge and sway magnificently in the tropical breeze. The tree produces only one bud with 100 fruits. Before it dies it shoots off a few new plants that grow with their single bud and 100 fruits. In the same time, the papaya tree has produced four bumper crops and keeps on giving, producing more sweet and juicy fruits.

Listening in the breeze, the banana tree sings: "I may have taken some time, I may have but one bud before I die, but look see, how beautiful. My life's purpose, 100 fruits with three new trees following me, the next generation to bear fruit."

The banana tree doesn't compare itself to or try to be the papaya tree. It produces one bud, 100 fruits and hands on to the next generation. May the banana tree inspire us to stand tall, share the fruits of our purpose and seed the pathway for the next generation.

Your True Essence is Front and Centre

We are all born with a true nature and purpose, as unique as your fingerprint it is held within your heart. You have all the gifts and talents within you to develop to bring the full flourishing of your true essence and purpose into the world.

Your true nature is your inner being, your essence. It is the vibration, the energy you emanate in a natural, relaxed state. Your essence may be inspirational, welcoming, joyful, generous, accepting, peaceful, strong, liberating, mischievous. This is the experience people, including the audience of your True Business, have with you. As the wise and powerful woman, Maya Angelou said:

> 'People may not remember exactly what you did, or what you said, but they will always remember how you made them feel.'

It is vital to be conscious of your true nature, your essence, as this naturally serves your audience to thrive. You want your true essence front and centre to pour your true essence through your business, your offering, brand and all communication such as website, social media, books, videos. This way, wherever you show up to interact authentically with your audience, your True Self is leading and present.

Sexologist and coach, Madalaine Monro's essence is gentleness. She is 'The Gentle Alchemist'. This natural gentleness inspires safety and acceptance, which serves her purpose of healing through pleasure in the fields of relationships and sexuality beautifully.

My personal experience of Madalaine, both in person and in her communication on Instagram, is that her gentle essence invites me to relax, soften, to be more present. I experience gentle alchemy simply from Madalaine showing up as her True Self. Her gentle true essence is her superpower.

My true essence is inspiring and invitational. My clients describe being ignited, energised and released, free to be themselves. This is the essence I want to consciously embody and pour through my True Business and all communication.

Before stepping into client sessions, workshops and meetings, I close my eyes, take a deep breath and evoke my true essence front and centre: "I am inspirational clarity and warm invitation, here to open up new pathways of the heart so that we are free to fulfil our purpose and humanity thrives."

In traditional business there are many occasions when we hide our true nature - when we are stressed, overwhelmed, frightened or anxious; or if we are frustrated, angry, disillusioned. You may be working in a culture that is competitive, manipulative or highly political, so present as cold, aloof and overly professional to protect yourself. You may be fearful about making enough money, and in response present as pushy, or desperate as you try to force through a sale.

When your true essence is hidden, masked by stress or protection, this can confuse or repel your audience and you gather this as evidence - 'I told you so! No one wants me, or what I have.' In this moment, your audience is robbed of the gift of your true essence that is a powerful contribution to them. Business becomes an uphill struggle.

During a period of my career when I was over working and significantly stressed, my inspirational essence became overshadowed by an impatient, frustrated, dictatorial leadership style. "I am inspiring and invitational" became "I am tired, busy and don't have time for this ****." People experienced me as abrupt, intimidating, rude, a far distance from my encouraging, playful and inspirational true nature. It was time to stop, reconnect to my heart and my true nature.

In a moment, we will connect with your true essence, so that you can make a conscious choice to place your true nature front and centre in your business, for your inner being to lead. Your true essence is exactly what your audience needs. It is a natural gift that serves them to evolve, grow and ultimately thrive.

Your Purpose is your North Star

Your purpose is your reason for being, your soul's calling, why you are here on earth and in business at this moment in time. When you choose to make your purpose your business, your business becomes a vehicle for your purpose and potential fulfilled, for making a meaningful contribution to the wider world.

I AM inspirational clarity, here to open new pathways of the heart in business that bring connection, happiness and wellness for us and the earth.

With your purpose as your North Star, you can delight in the quiet confidence of knowing who you are and what you are here for; you benefit from the energy that clarity of focus and direction brings.

Decision making is made easier as you ask, does it take me closer to or further away from my purpose? On the occasions self-doubt creeps in; when you find yourself caught in the day-to-day; overwhelmed by the to-do list; or intimidated by a game-changing meeting recalling your purpose, your North Star, restores your focus. As you clearly and consistently communicate your purpose, your audience becomes inspired and engaged and your business grows.

Maddy Cooper, is a founding partner of UK marketing agency, Brilliant Noise. Burned out from the pressure of focusing on financial targets leaving her cold; and running an agency through the pandemic combined with home-schooling a three-year-old and six-year-old, Maddy had lost enthusiasm for her business. She also felt as if she'd lost touch with what she was good at. She wanted her new True Business!

As Maddy listened to her heart's wisdom, her true purpose emerged – a deep and urgent desire to protect the earth for her family, for all families, so they have a bright future.

This is her purpose, inspiring her to become a leader of sustainability marketing; to lead difficult conversations and action to create genuinely sustainable and regenerative business. Passionately against green-washing - where businesses use marketing to persuade the public that an organisation is environmentally friendly - Maddy wanted to seek out and work with global leaders who genuinely care and are ready and willing to take urgent action.

Maddy's true purpose brought fire and focus and the energy and love for her business returned tenfold. She educated herself with a sustainability course at Cambridge University and wrote a sustainability marketing manifesto for Brilliant Noise. She wrote opinion pieces and articles for marketing industry press; and hosted round table discussions for 150 plus fellow marketers leading the debate, pressing for urgent unified action. She led the Brilliant Noise pitch to win the BMW account just in time for Christmas, Nike, Allianz and Molson Coors shortly after.

With devotion to her purpose and urgency to meet 2030 climate targets Maddy has now set up a new sustainability marketing agency, Flourish, dedicated to global brands accelerating their sustainability transformation and reaping the commercial rewards. She is spearheading the *Marketing Declares a Climate Emergency* movement, in collaboration with the BIMA Sustainability Council, to lead the entire marketing industry into sustainability transformation.

Charles Hoskinson is a US entrepreneur, co-founder of Ethereum and Cardano blockchains. His purpose is to reinvent the global financial system to shift financial power from one government or financial institution back to the people.

Charles shares his vision to roll out the Cardano blockchain across Africa, putting corruption-free, financial power back into the hands of the African people, to build a financial system that rights the wrongs of slavery. This deeply inspiring purpose and vision has engaged one of the biggest and most loyal audiences and communities in the cryptocurrency space who have invested billions of dollars into Cardano.

Seven Stages of Purpose

Your purpose doesn't arrive one day - 'boom!' - fully formed, expressed, embodied at the heart of your business and life, it emerges and evolves.

Simon Haas, yoga philosopher and author of *'The Book of Dharma: Making Enlightened Choices'*, shares that when you live your true nature, your purpose emerges naturally over time. He goes into depth about the stages of purpose in his second book *'Yoga and the Dark Night of the Soul'*.

There are recognisable stages to making your purpose your business. You may experience more than one stage at a time. Some stages last longer than others, you may go round the different stages many times. When you become aware of the stage you are at, you can consciously participate in the emergence of your purpose at the heart of your business.

Calling – Led by a desire for more meaning, you begin to sense you have a purpose bigger than what is currently being expressed. There may be a sense of 'something' missing, a frustration, a pulling you towards 'something' you can't articulate or understand. We can stay here for years unless we consciously acknowledge the calling and allow it to emerge.

Receive – Ask your heart to reveal your true purpose and choose to listen and receive it. The more you acknowledge and follow your true nature, the more your purpose will emerge and the clearer it becomes.

Articulate – On following your true nature and receiving your purpose you reach a point where you can clearly and simply articulate your purpose in a way that inspires you and your audience. The simpler the better. For example, Teen Yoga exists to empower young people with yoga.

Align – Now your purpose is clearly articulated, consciously make business decisions in alignment with your purpose. Let go of any aspect of the business not aligned with your purpose to create space for what is. As you practice alignment your clarity and commitment grow.

Embody – After making decisions aligned with your purpose for a period of time, your purpose grows from being an intellectual understanding to become a tangible, living expression. You embody your true nature and purpose and are becoming a living, breathing expression of your purpose in the world.

Lead – With the embodiment of your true nature and purpose, you are 'walking your talk'. Your integrity, substance and depth of experience and mastery inspire others and you become a sought after leader in your field.

Evolution – Your true nature and purpose is a living evolutionary force in your business and life, bringing a quantum leap of growth to a new chapter.

Katherine Woodward Thomas is the best-selling author of *'Calling in "The One": 7 Weeks to Attract the Love of Your Life.'* A family and marriage counsellor, Katherine developed a pioneering metaphysical process to call in your love match. She used this process to call in her life partner at 42 and they had a child together.

A leader in her field, Katherine served thousands of people to create their love match and trained hundreds of *Calling in "The One"* coaches, speaking at international symposiums with her peers Marianne Williamson, Deepak Chopra, Neale Donald Walsch.

Then Katherine separated from her husband - Her One! She speaks candidly about the vulnerability of the separation, alongside the fear for her business built around *Calling in "The One".*

Led by her purpose, which she describes as 'serving the thrust of love into the universe', she was guided to separate from her husband with love. *'Conscious Uncoupling: 5 Steps to Living Happily Even After'* became her second book. She laughs that this wasn't the book she wanted to write! *Conscious Uncoupling* became a New York Times bestseller, made famous by actress Gwyneth Paltrow and singer Chris Martin consciously uncoupling.

While a traditional business may have folded, Katherine led by her purpose, her North Star, stepped into a significant growth period of evolution in service to Love.

Guided Meditation

Discover Your True Essence and Purpose

This is your time to listen to your heart, to dive into the wisdom and creativity it holds. To ask and receive your essence and purpose so you can intentionally make this your True Business, it is what you were born to do.

Give yourself this time and space to receive the inspiration, nourishment and potent transformation your heart's wisdom and creativity bring. From the inspiration you receive, you can articulate your purpose clearly and simply to inspire and engage you and your audience.

Be curious and welcome in the experience. Play freely. Allow for the unexpected as you are guided on the journey. You don't need to make anything happen in your imagination, simply be present and receive, notice what emerges. Remember you can also download and listen to these meditations at katbyles.com.

Turn off any distractions and get comfortable. Feel your feet on the floor and your back supported by the chair. Take a deep breath into your belly and out. Bring your awareness to your thoughts, watch your mind, notice what is going on for you right now, be the compassionate observer, no judgement. What feelings are your thoughts generating?

Bring your awareness to your body, noticing sensations, areas of tightness or clenching. Bring your attention to your head, inviting a softening, your cheeks, nose, ears and jaw. Down through your neck and throat, softening. Drop your shoulders, and invite a softening through your torso, arms and hands. Softening down through your pelvis, hips to your legs, knees, ankles, feet and toes.

Notice your sitting bones making contact with the chair. Feel the chair rising up to support and hold you. You can let go and allow yourself to experience being held by the chair, by the earth, for a moment. Breathe in loving kindness from the soles of your feet all the way up through your body. Every single cell of your body and being receiving the energy of loving kindness.

Now step into innocence, the bridge into your heart, where you can listen deeply to your inner wisdom and come into harmony with Source, the infinite creative energy of the universe.

Let your imagination take you to a beautiful beach. Feel your feet on the soft, white sand and the gentle, warm sunshine on your face. Take a breath. Turquoise sea stretches to the horizon and the waves gently lap on the shore. Immersed in the beauty and wonder all around, choose to receive your true essence and purpose.

You are drawn to the back of the beach. You can see lush tropical vegetation and two palm trees leaning towards each other forming an entrance to a pathway through the rainforest. You set off up the beach towards them, feeling the warm sand underfoot, gentle sunshine on your back. As you reach the palm trees you may like to run your hands over the bark, feeling the texture, as you step underneath them and onto the pathway that is beckoning you forward.

Wandering along the path, you are curious, open and deeply receptive. Taking in the beauty around you: this lush tropical forest is humming with life.

You begin to notice the sounds around you and can hear running water in the distance. As you walk along the pathway, it gets louder until the path joins and runs alongside a stream. Notice how clear the water is as it dances over the rocks, making its way to the ocean. You can step down to the stream and cup your hands to taste water. You may like to wash your hands, face, back of your neck. The freshness of the air clears your mind and energy, sweeping away anything in your energy field that no longer serves you.

Setting off again along the path, you notice up ahead it opens into a clearing. Here you find yourself standing on lush green dewy grass, blue sky above you and colourful birds flying between the trees. Your attention is drawn to the waterfall tumbling into the crystal-clear rock pool. This is the Pool of your Essence, your true nature, your inner being.

As you stand by the pool, it begins to bubble from the depths. As the bubbles reach the surface, they form a word that describes your true essence. Simply be with the bubbling for a moment until a word that describes your inner being forms.

Make your way into the pool. Dive in from the rocks, wade in from the shallows, glide in from the side. Fully immerse yourself under the water, in your true essence, you can breathe and swim easily. Every single cell of your being comes into harmony with your true essence, your true nature.

As you make your way to the surface of the water, taking in the beauty and wonder of the natural world all around you, you say the "I AM..." followed by the word or words describing your true essence. Breath in the vibration and energy of each word, let it fill you up.

Say the words "HERE TO..." and the words describing your purpose follow. Listen. Breathe them in.

Say the words "SO THAT..." and listen to your heart's response.

"I AM... HERE TO... SO THAT..."

Take a moment to lie back on the water held by your essence and purpose, allowing it to settle into your body.When you are ready, swim to the edge of the pool where there are some natural steps formed in the rocks for you to climb out easily.

Finding your feet back on the lush green grass, warm sunshine on your skin, you notice the water droplets begin to evaporate. Notice how you feel standing here with your essence and purpose spilling forth from your heart.

Now on the earth in front of you, draw a golden circle. This is your heart's vision of your purpose fulfilled. Step in and receive your heart's vision of your purpose fulfilled. What is life like for you, for others, for planet earth with your purpose fulfilled? Be here for a moment breathing it in.

So it is, so it shall be.

Take a deep breath. Begin to wriggle your fingers and your toes. When you are ready, bring yourself gently back into the room. Pick up your pen and write about your true essence, purpose, and the vision of your purpose fulfilled. Let the inspiration continue to pour through your writing until you feel complete. Take this inspiration from your heart and articulate your purpose clearly and simply.

Journal

Dive a little deeper into your true nature and purpose. Journal for 20 minutes around the following questions:

1. What do you love about your true nature and purpose?
2. What elements of your business are not in alignment with your purpose?
3. What are you ready to let go of to make space for what is in alignment?
4. Is anything blocking you choosing your true nature and purpose in business?
5. What reality does your true purpose open up for you, your audience, the world?
6. Imagine your purpose fulfilled, what are you most proud of?
7. What is one action to take today in alignment with your true nature and purpose?
8. Think of a decision to make, what takes you closer to your purpose?

A little note as you receive the truth of who you are and what you are here for - watch for your ego's reaction. You may want to dismiss your essence and purpose as too much, not enough, not right, or pretend it's not you. Simply acknowledge this as resistance, your ego's reaction. It's okay.

In the morning, before you begin your business day, breathe in your true essence and purpose: "I AM, HERE TO, SO THAT." Breathe it in before important meetings, phone calls, presentations, difficult conversations. Make decisions that take you closer to your true nature and purpose. As you do and you begin to embody your true nature and purpose, this becomes the norm, your ego's reaction falls away.

Your True Business blueprint is now underway. You are acquainted with the essence that deeply serves and your purpose for being here on earth and in business. Now let's explore who your true nature and purpose naturally serve to thrive. Let's welcome in your audience.

CHAPTER 4

WELCOME IN YOUR AUDIENCE

"Being of service to others is what brings true happiness."
- Marie Osmond

There are two plum trees in Crabbe Hill Village. The first is next to the roadside and this year it has a bumper crop of juicy plums. My partner Trevor tells me the plum tree must be at least 100 years old because as a kid, he used to sit in the tree and fill his belly with ripe plums. This makes me happy that we spent a day freeing the plum tree from the undergrowth suffocating and killing it. It lives on.

The second plum tree is tucked away on the hillside and has a smaller crop of the sweetest, sweet plums. They are almost a different fruit. These are the plums for me, sweet, sweet, sweetness, bathed in all-day sunshine and sweeping sea views. No other people or birds stop to eat these. A best kept secret, protected by the convenient and easily reachable plums by the road.

This is just like you in your business. Your unique essence naturally attracts and serves your audience who come to you for this gift. Show up and be yourself for your audience, the people you love and want to see thrive.

Who Are You Naturally Here to Serve?

In traditional business, you identify a target audience. You identify a need amongst a particular group of people and with it a financial opportunity for your business. You explain, convince, manipulate them into believing they need the product or service you have with marketing, advertising and make the sale.

In your True Business, your true essence and purpose naturally serve your audience to thrive. It is a perfect match, a win-win.

If your true essence is gentleness and your purpose is to heal through pleasure, this will naturally benefit couples or individuals recovering from hurt or trauma. If your true essence is magnificence and generosity, your purpose to protect the earth for future generations, this is of significant value to legacy brands who have done harm and want to change; to global brands who want to lead urgent and real sustainable change now.

'Everyone is my audience' is a common mistake. There are 8 billion people on planet earth! Everyone is not your audience. 'It's women' – there's 4 billion of those. Is it women solo travellers;

women healing from divorce; women CEO's who burn out; women taking up painting; women learning plumbing; women who have just become mums; women who want to cook plant-based recipes; women navigating menopause; women leading ocean education and restoration? Be clear so you can take a stand for your audience and speak clearly and directly to them. Show up for them and own and communicate clearly the value and transformation you bring.

Your heart's wisdom will reveal to you the people your essence and purpose naturally serve; the people that you bring real, soulful value to help them thrive, prosper and progress. This will be a group of people you love and want to invest your life force, wisdom creative energy in. When this becomes clear, listen and get to know them deeply, their challenges, needs, visions, hopes and dreams.

When we are not serving our true audience - perhaps we are chasing the money, or if in the US, staying in a job because it comes with health insurance, or taking a fill-in position to acquire funds and courage before we move into our True Business - we can feel a buzz, a charge from achieving. However, being out of alignment over time is unsustainable and eventually we become depleted and drained. We struggle to keep going, to get clients, to get up in the morning. We may feel as if we don't belong, lose confidence and belief in our purpose.

During a discovery session, I connected with a woman in Australia who had invested $10,000 with an executive coach to create an e-book targeting corporate coaching clients because "that's where the money is." The investment had yielded zero return. There was nothing in the pipeline and she was beginning to panic.

Listening to her heart we both received her audience, the people her true nature and purpose serves as 'the youth of Australia'. She opened up about a game she had invented for teenagers to build their self-esteem and resilience. She lit up and the inspiration flooded through her so much so that I still remember the conversation many years later. Teenagers, not corporations, were the audience for her True Business. Sadly, she was so knocked back by the experience of chasing a target audience in the wrong direction, that in that moment she didn't have the courage to switch and follow the path of her heart.

Once you know your audience, speak directly to them. Based in Australia, Marie McAneny, founder of Heart of Nursing, was a nurse in a hospital environment where bullying, blame and burn-out were the norm. Marie was keen to change this by empowering nurses with leadership programmes. She approached hospital management and the lack of interest was causing self-doubt to creep in, undermining her purpose to support nurses on the front line caring for others.

Marie's heart invited her to shift her focus, bypass hospital management and speak directly to nurses. Inspired, within a few weeks, Marie created and piloted a workshop called 'Soul Medicine for Nurses' which she ran for small groups in retreat centres and spas. Marie loves cruises, so she had the inspired idea to host Soul Medicine for Nurses on a cruise to the Whitsunday Islands. 80 nurses signed up in four days. This simple shift to focus her love and energy on nurses, her true audience, transformed Marie's business from stuck to flow and sold out.

The Message of your Heart

When you know who your true audience is, what do you most want to say to them, from your heart to theirs?

In traditional business, you design a message to sell, influence or inform your target audience. You identify the language used by the target audience to make the message relatable and say what they want to hear to direct them towards a particular outcome. Your message has an agenda to serve the end result you want.

Rarely heart-led, however, politics can demonstrate the importance of your message. It is politicians with a clear message that win elections. Barack Obama: "Yes We Can." Donald Trump: "Make America Great Again." Can you remember John McCain's or Hillary Clinton's message? No, because it didn't get through or they didn't have one.

The message of your True Business comes directly from your heart and speaks clearly, simply to the heart of your audience. It has a resonance of love, truth and inspiration that cuts through noise and ego manipulation. It creates real connection and thriving for all.

Tanya Smith is a Leadership and Change Catalyst based in Canada with a purpose to empower people to be leaders of their own lives. Tanya's logical thinking mind suggested the message: "I empower to you to fly." Notice the emphasis on 'I', a contradiction.

When Tanya listened to her heart, the message she wants to share with her true audience is: "You were born for Greatness." Boom! It speaks directly to the heart, to the heart of Tanya's audience.

Your heart's message is also what YOU most need to hear. You are the first customer and, if you allow it, your heart's message will take you and your business on a journey of transformation beyond your imagination. Because of this power held in your heart's message you may be tempted to reject it, rubbish it, dismiss it or dilute it. Don't. Let it work its magic on you.

Initially, I rejected my heart's message "Follow your Heart" as a cliché! However, as I slowly embraced it, it has been one of the most transformational, creative periods of my life, opening up a new frontier of business brimming with happiness, abundance and vitality.

A note too that I was also afraid business leaders would reject my message: 'Heart isn't businessy!' Then the realisation that my audience isn't traditional business leaders chasing profit. It is creative leaders who want to do business differently. Who want to open up new pathways in alignment with our true nature, the Earth and Source, universal energy. To this group of people, 'Follow your Heart' is met with relief and deep appreciation.

Once your heart's message becomes clear and rings deeply true for you, you can build a story around it. Gather substance to illustrate it with case studies, research, statistics, endorsements and your own personal experience. Then share it to inspire your audience at every opportunity consistently and confidently.

At the Homeless World Cup, which has a purpose to beat homelessness with football, we consistently and confidently shared the message 'Sport Changes Lives' with our players, spectators, partners, media, sponsors, donors, volunteers and governments.

We illustrated this message with powerful stories of players beating drug addiction, moving into new homes, becoming coaches, leaders in their communities and even playing for their national team. Our impact report shared statistics such as '77% of players positively changed their lives'. High-profile leaders such as Nelson Mandela's statement that 'Sport has the power to change the world' added gravity as did endorsements for the Homeless World Cup from Eric Cantona, Desmond Tutu and Lewis Hamilton.

This powerful messaging and story grew the organisation's impact from 20 to 70 nations reaching 250,000 people who were homeless to positively change their lives in just five years. It engaged players to trust, step into the fire and transform their lives; partners and sponsors to fund the foundation; ambassadors to support with their voices and platform; spectators to drop stereotypes and support with gusto. Messaging from the heart is magical, powerful and transformational for everyone it touches.

The Optimal Channel to Reach your Audience

Where are you showing up to reach your audience and share your inspirational message with them? To confidently and consistently add the value of your true nature, purpose and message to your audience.

Many small business owners make the mistake of believing you have to be everywhere. You feel the pressure to build an all singing, all dancing website, feature daily on social media –

Facebook, Twitter, Instagram, TikTok, YouTube, LinkedIn – write articles, feature on podcasts, appear on national media – TV, radio, magazines, online. Build an email list, write a book, speak on the stage, host workshops and make films and videos! More than a full-time job, this is a communications strategy for a team of five and a budget of £20,000 per month.

Attempting to cover all communication bases is unrealistic and unnecessary and will only cause overwhelm, frustration, disappointment and ultimately failure. You will be inconsistent, scattered all over the place and have little impact. Your audience will be left not knowing where to find you. Unless you have the team and budget to deliver this, attempting this is a form of self-sabotage.

Your heart's wise inner compass knows the optimal channel for you to reach and grow your audience. For Bex Shindler, founder of The Mindful Kitchen, it was Facebook Lives to teach plant--based cookery classes. For personal finance blogger Mrs MummyPenny it is UK national media to share ways to clear debt, save and become financially savvy. Writer JK Rowling shows up on Twitter to speak out about issues close to her heart.

At the Homeless World Cup we showed up consistently in global media, including film (feature films, documentaries, short films, promotional films), TV, newspapers, magazines, radio and online sharing the message, sport changes lives. We grew our audience to support 250,000 people to transform their lives with 70 national partners and raise £2 million+ each year within five years.

Your logical mind or ego may have one idea of the best channel of communication to reach your audience and your heart a completely different one. Listen to your heart as connection is the most expansive, alive, impactful and fulfilling here.

Simon Haas is the yoga philosopher and teacher, author of 'The Book of Dharma' and 'Yoga and the Dark Night of the Soul'. His purpose is to make ancient wisdom accessible in modern day life for yoga teachers and people living a spiritual path.

Simon wanted to write articles and blogs for magazines and receive book reviews. He is a writer after all. However, when we connected with his heart, we both experienced a vision of him speaking at festivals to thousands: his soul family. Speaking on the stage is his optimal channel of communication.

Simon is an introvert, a quiet, considered scholar, so speaking was not an obvious first choice, but his heart had clearly spoken. Each time I called a yoga magazine to propose an article or book review, they asked if Simon would speak at an upcoming festival or event! His heart was opening up opportunities for him to step into.

Within a few weeks, Simon had a three-month UK tour with 12 speaking engagements scheduled. Invitations from France, Lithuania, the Netherlands and Costa Rica followed. Two years on, Simon was invited to speak at the United Nations for the International Day of Yoga before going on to a workshop for thousands at a yoga festival in Mexico.

Simon is living his heart's expansive vision, doing effortlessly what he'd previously believed would be challenging. He wrote the articles and received book reviews too, but it was speaking from his heart to his soul family that brought significant growth and book sales.

You can't cut and paste a marketing template or borrow someone else's communications strategy that successfully yielded results for them. You have to follow the path of your own heart. So before you invest thousands of pounds and hours in a course teaching you how to Podcast, YouTube or Speak on the stage, or with a PR company to secure media coverage, or any other channel, make sure you first connect with your heart and align with your truly optimal channel of communication.

Steph Magenta, founder of Integrative Breath, breathwork facilitator and shamanic teacher, is naturally gifted at Facebook and Instagram. Her presence is palpable and she shows up consistently, serving her audience with inspiration and value.

Steph set up a Facebook group for a 21-day breathwork challenge, with an expectation that 50 friends may join. Over 1000 people participated and breathwork teachers from around the world volunteered to contribute different classes each day. Steph found herself at the centre of the breathwork field as an advocate and teacher, and her breathwork facilitation trainings sold out.

Suzie Poyser, a psychiatrist and counsellor, trained with Steph to become a Breathwork facilitator, setting up the 'Breathe Back to Calm' program to help people address anxiety. Suzie adopted Steph's optimal channel of communication – social media – to reach her audience. Only Suzie had no desire at all to be on Instagram or Facebook and felt like she was hustling with no impact.

Suzie's heart shared her optimal channel to reach her audiences is through businesses, not social media. She switched her focus to align with her heart. Within a few weeks, Suzie's zero impact rose to serving a thousand people a week to restore their wellness in the workplace.

As you master your optimal channel of communication and become a consistent, valuable presence to your growing audience over a number of years, momentum builds. Now you may spill into new channels of communication without effort.

Joe Wicks, The Body Coach, is a UK personal trainer on a mission to get the world fitter, stronger, healthier and happier. He has grown his audience by showing up on Instagram sharing HIIT workouts, recipes and before and after transformation photos of his clients on the 90-day programme. Joe's first Instagram post had one comment from his Mum encouraging him. By showing up consistently for 10 years, Joe has grown his Instagram audience to 5 million people.

During the coronavirus pandemic, the UK entered a period of lockdown and Joe announced on Instagram that he would be providing daily PE lessons for children and adults stuck at home live on YouTube. It caught the imagination of national and global media who shared the story. Run an internet search for PE with Joe, Joe Wicks and you will find over 15,000 news articles around the world.

After showing up every day live on YouTube for 18 weeks, Fridays in fancy dress, Joe became a household name with nearly 3 million YouTube subscribers. PE with Joe received over 70 million YouTube views, broke the record for the number of people on a live broadcast and was one of the top YouTube videos in the UK for 2020. He donated over £500,000 made from the YouTube channel to NHS Charities.

As Joe's business built around his calling to get people mentally and physically fit grew in momentum, it spilled from Instagram into books, YouTube, national and global media. When Joe launched The Body Coach App, billboard advertising and outdoor media was also included and national press reported that the Body Coach App generated £9 million in revenue in the first week alone. Through all of this Instagram remains Joe's optimal channel to inspire and build relationships on a daily basis.

Guided Meditation

Welcome in your Audience

Let's welcome in and meet your true audience, receive your heart's message and optimal channel of communication.

Find yourself a quiet, comfortable spot where you won't be interrupted for a guided meditation, turn off any distractions and bring your pen and paper.

When you are ready, take a seat, feel your feet on the floor, back supported, and gently close your eyes. Take a deep breath into your belly and out. Become aware of your thoughts and feelings, notice what thoughts and feelings your mind is generating in relation to your audience, 'I'll never reach them, do I even have an audience, why would anyone listen to me etc.' No judgement, simply observe.

Now bring your awareness into your body, noticing any sensations, any tension in the body. Invite in relaxation through your head, jaw, throat. Drop your shoulders and relax down through your arms and hands. Relax through your torso, spine, solar plexus, let your belly out. Feel your sitting bones in contact with the chair and relax down through your legs, feet and toes. Take a deep breath and breathe loving kindness into the whole of your body. Send loving kindness to the audience your true nature and purpose naturally serves.

Next, step into innocence, the bridge into your heart, where you can listen deeply to your heart's wisdom and align with Source universal energy.

Let your imagination take you back to the Pool of your Essence. Find yourself in the clearing with the waterfall cascading into the pool, feet on the lush green grass, blue sky above the trees. Every single cell of your being comes into harmony with the magnificence of life here. Take in the wonder and notice you are grounded, open and curious.

You jump, dive, glide or wade into the water, into the pool of Essence, and immerse yourself fully in the water. You can breathe freely underwater and you immerse yourself fully into your true nature and purpose, your I AM, HERE TO, SO THAT.

Swimming in the Pool of your Essence, invite in your audience, the people that your essence and purpose naturally serve. Welcome them, say hello and how happy you are to see them, to be with them.

Notice who they are, observe what is obvious about them. What life stage, issue or situation are they facing? Observe the impact of your essence and purpose.

Ask your audience: What is it that you need? Listen to the response.

Ask: What value do you receive from working with me? Listen to their response. What do you love about working with me? Again, listen to their response.

Ask: What transformation do you experience working with me? Listen.

Notice what happens if you don't show up for your audience.

Your audience is invited to enjoy relaxing in this beautiful space while you swim to the edge of the pool. You see there are natural steps carved into the edge so you can easily climb out on to the side, lush green grass under your feet: you can feel the warmth of the sunshine on your skin.

Standing here, your true nature and purpose consistently serving your audience, building relationships, draw a golden circle on the earth in front of you. This is your heart's message, the one thing your heart wants to say to your audience. Step into the golden circle and receive your heart's message. Feel the vibration of the transmission. Ask your heart to share the words with you. Take a moment to fully receive it, before stepping back into the clearing with your Essence Pool and waterfall, your feet on the earth.

You notice that the waterfall has slightly parted and you can now see a cave behind it which you walk towards, curious, open and deeply receptive.

You walk into the cave that feels calm and safe. You may be able to see different colours, gems, markings on the cave walls. To the back of the cave there is a light that draws you towards it, this is an opening and portal through to you reaching your audience in your optimal channel of communication to reach your audience.

Step through and find yourself effortlessly connecting with and growing your audience in your channel. Where are you? What are you doing? What is created when you show up here consistently? What does the connection with your audience feel like? Drink it all in.

Share your message with your audience, along with the energy of the transmission. Notice the impact it has and what it opens up for your audience. Take a moment here to be together with this inspiring message and its impact.

When you are ready, in your own time, open your eyes and come back into the room. Take a moment to make any notes and continue to receive the inspiration and alignment with your audience, inspirational message from your heart to theirs and channel of communication until you feel complete.

Journal

Let's journal to connect more deeply with your audience and begin to assimilate and align with your message and channel to reach them.

1. What qualities do you love about your audience?
2. What value and transformation do you bring to your audience?

3. What is your audience and the world denied if you don't show up?
4. What does your heart's message inspire in you and your audience?
5. What is your ego's reaction and relationship to your heart's message?
6. What opens up when you show up consistently in your channel of communication?
7. What skills do you need to acquire to master your channel of communication?
8. What is one inspired action for you to take today to serve your audience?

Now you are welcoming in and getting to know your audience, what is your Heart's Offering for them? This is the product or service that delivers the highest value to your audience, fulfils your purpose and provides a financial income, a win-win.

CHAPTER 5

DESIGN YOUR HEART'S OFFERING

"Marketing is what you do when your product is no good."
- Edwin H Land, Founder, Polaroid

Summer in Antigua is the most beautiful time of the year. The turquoise sea becomes still and crystal clear, offering up divine swimming. Banana, papaya, mango, sugar apple, soursop, melon, lemon, and coconuts spill forth on village trees, ripening in warm sunshine.

Eating a sweet, juicy mango immersed in salty Caribbean waters with morning sunshine on your face is heavenly.

This is the Caribbean Nature's offering in abundance. Just like this, we all have an offering ready to spill forth from our heart, naturally nourishing and serving our audience and world to thrive.

Your Heart's Offering Delivers Value and Revenue

When you connect to your heart's wisdom and receive your true nature and purpose, the most common question that follow is: 'How is that a business?' 'How will I make money from my purpose?' The answer is with your Heart's Offering.

Your Heart's Offering, your signature product or service, is the way in which you serve your audience with value, fulfil your purpose and receive financial reward. When your offering is created from your heart, it holds the highest value for your audience, you and the wider world.

Like a chef's signature dish, your Heart's Offering is a unique and distinctive blend of your true nature and purpose, talents and gifts, life experiences, training and learnings. As it delivers real, lasting value to your audience it creates loyalty and word-of-mouth referrals. It sets you apart in your field as a leading authority, making you visible and sought after. No convincing, cajoling or manipulative marketing is required.

The beauty of your offering is that you are the first customer, giving you a deep and real understanding of the value, impact and joy it brings to others, because first you receive all that value yourself.

Joe Wicks, The Body Coach, is on a mission to get you moving to feel fitter, happier and healthier. His original offering was 'The 90 Day Programme', a three-step online course of HIIT videos and recipes tailored to you for around £90. It has since progressed to The Body Coach App for a monthly or annual fee.

Joe's product delivers his clients into physical and mental fitness with impressive results, fulfilling his purpose. The physical and mental transformation turns his clients into walking adverts. Because of the results, because Joe cares, because Joe walks his talk, The Body Coach customers are loyal. They champion Joe and refer friends and family to him.

Katherine Woodward Thomas is the US-based marriage and family psychotherapist with a purpose of serving the thrust of love into the universe. Her Heart's Offering is the best-selling book: *"Calling in "The One": 7 Week to Attract the Love of your Life'.* These are the principles with which Katheriune created her partner with whom she shares a daughter. Katherine was the first customer.

Katherine has since been interviewed by CNN, New York Times, Wall Street Journal and Washington Post and shared the stage with her peers Marianne Williamson, Alanis Morrissette and Deepak Chopra. In an industry of thousands of relationship counsellors, Katherine's Heart's Offering has ensured her rise to stand out as the pioneer she is, the go-to person to prepare to receive your love match and live a life enriched with love.

Developing your Heart's Offering

Your Heart's Offering is your life's best work, the greatest gift you can offer to your audience. Pour your love and care into your offering and craft it with devotion. Inspiration may pour through in one go, or take time to emerge and develop. Listen for the inspiration, play and experiment, create and adjust.

What form will your offering take? A book, course, programme, retreat, a song, a painting, sculpture, poetry, a performance. Perhaps it's blockchain technology, software, a mobile app, a wedding cake, organic skin care, high performance sportswear, a chair, a medical technique, pioneering therapy or healing practice?

Your offering delivers your purpose for your audience. On top of that, what specific end result does your offering create for your audience and the wider world? How does it make them feel? What is the price? What is the name? Connecting to your heart to explore and receive the answers to these key product development questions gives you a skeleton frame to build upon.

When you are clear of the end results, you work backwards, designing your product to facilitate these end results for your audience and fulfil your purpose. Test, pilot, observe the impact. Adjust your product guided by your heart's wisdom until your Heart's offering delivers the end results to your audience and wider world you want it to, until it is your life's best work.

Pricing your Heart's Offering

Pricing your Heart's Offering can be a minefield, triggering unconscious wounds around your value and worth, not being good enough, causing you to under or overprice your offering. This does a disservice to yourself and your audience.

Base your pricing on the value you bring to your audience; the financial amount your audience can meet and what you'd love to receive. Check this against any industry pricing standard?

If the price feels too high to you, you may have a tendency to discount. Instead, grow in the understanding the value of your Heart's Offering and communicate this to your audience confidently and clearly. Once you understand and acclimatise to the real value your Heart's Offering brings, you may realise the price is a bargain!

If the price feels too low to you, you may have a product mix with additional products provided at a higher price point; or your offering may be destined for a large mainstream audience and you are dealing in a large number of sales. For example, Joe Wicks, The Body Coach App is around £90 to transform your body, improve your mental health and create new habits for a lifetime. This is incredible value. The price makes it affordable and accessible to hundreds of thousands of people.

There has been a trend for coaches of putting up prices significantly. If you decide to put your prices up significantly, be aware you will most likely need to build a new audience for the new price structure. Make sure you dedicate the time and resources to do that.

What about discounting? Brands such as Apple never discount. There is one clear and consistent price across all Apple shops and resellers, which, when accompanied by consistent quality, is unquestioned. There are brands that discount twice a year that long-term customers look out for. There are also brands that make discounts available all year round. My experience is that constant discounting undermines the product. Why would you pay full price for a product if you know there will be a sale shortly?

Keep it simple. Connect with your heart's wisdom, step beyond ego agendas, uncomfortable thoughts and feelings, and receive the price of your Heart's Offering that is honouring of the value and impact it brings to you, your audience and the world. This is a sweet spot where the value meets your idea of a fair exchange and an amount your audience is happy to pay. Trust that.

Your Product Mix

Over time your Heart's Offering may be presented in more than one format, producing a product mix that serves your audience at different price points.

Calling in "The One" by Katherine Woodward Thomas was originally presented as a book to prepare to welcome in your love match, priced at $12. A couple of years later, Katherine launched a 7-week online course that allowed thousands of people all over the world to work in person with Katherine to create their love match, which was priced at $297.

Then came a 6-month training programme to become a *Calling in "The One"* coach, which enabled relationship counsellors and coaches to learn the *Calling in "The One"* methodology priced at $7,995. This is a comprehensive *Calling in "The One"* product mix all focused on preparing for your Love Match and living a life with love fulfilling Katherine's purpose of serving the thrust of love into the universe.

My Heart's Offering *'PR with Heart'*, to grow your audience and impact for a thriving business and world, is made available to creative leaders, teachers and healers who want to do business differently with an affordable and accessible investment via an online course priced at £300.

When clients want to add a board level communications director specialising in heart-led communication and business to their team one to one coaching begins at £3,000 for six months or The Antigua Retreat offers a creative business immersion in nature for pure source inspiration at £5,000 for a week.

Global organisations and leaders can work directly with me via consultancy to create and implement their heart-based communications strategy to scale their reach and impact sustainability from £5,000 per month.

All products fulfil my purpose of connecting creative leaders to their heart's wisdom and inspiration in business so that humanity thrives.

Traditional business will advise you to focus on creating the highest value offering first so you secure and bring in the largest amount of revenue. My invitation is to listen to your heart and what you are called to create now, where your inspiration, energy and eagerness lies. Go with this natural, powerful, Creative Flow.

With Katherine Woodward Thomas, it was the *'Calling in "The One"'* book that she created first, the lowest price point in the product mix. However, it was the book that brought the valuable Calling in "The One" intellectual property in to being that went on to become a purposeful and impactful product mix and a thriving business.

Guided Meditation

Design your Heart's Offering

This is the space and time for you to connect to your heart and pour its wisdom and creativity into your offering. To prepare, you may like to go for a walk in nature to clear your head, dance or move your body, clear your space of clutter, and settle into stillness.

Turn off distractions, get comfortable, and close your eyes. Take a deep breath. As you sit with the intention of designing your offering, bring awareness to your thoughts and feelings, no judgement. Bring your awareness into your body and if there are any areas in your body where you are holding tension, or clenching, you are invited to gently soften. Your head, jaw, shoulders, arms, torso, legs, feet. Feel your sitting bones in contact with the chair, your back supported.

Step into innocence, the bridge into your heart, where you can listen to your heart's wisdom and the fresh creative impulse and emergence of life through you now. Take yourself to the beautiful Pool of your Essence with the waterfall and stream that makes its way out into the ocean. Feel your feet on the earth, warm gentle sunshine on your face, your body relaxes even more. You can feel the humming of life here that is always serving your highest flourishing.

Choose to receive your Heart's Offering and dive into the Pool of your Essence. Feel the cool clear water on your skin, every cell of your being coming into harmony with your essence. As you dive down deep, you can breathe under water and there is a gift for you to create your Heart's Offering. Receive that now and bring it to the surface with you. As you do, you reconnect with your I AM… HERE TO… SO THAT… Breathe that in.

When you are ready, swim to the side of your Essence Pool where there are natural steps for you to climb out onto the lush green grass. Feeling the warmth on your skin and the vibration of your being standing in your true essence.

In your imagination, draw a beautiful golden circle on the earth. This represents the form your Heart's Offering takes. Step in and receive the form of your offering. Relax, receive it, welcome it in. The full flourishing of your heart's vision of the form of your offering, fulfilling your purpose, serving your audience, generating revenue.

Next draw a golden circle on the earth in front of you. This is the end result your offering creates for your audience. Step in and receive their end result. Standing in the vision, what is the value and transformation? What emotion do they experience?

Somewhere in this vision you are drawn to a golden label hanging down with the name of your offering written across it. What does it say? The price is listed on the other side. Turn it over. What does that say? Is there any other information?

Ask your heart to show you the end result your Heart's Offering creates for you and your business, for the world.

Take a moment to sit with your Heart's Offering, in the stillness, the form and end results it creates for you, your audience and the world, its name and pricing. So it is and so it shall be. What's the next obvious skilful action for you to take?

When you are ready, open your eyes and come back to the room. Take a moment to record your discoveries and keep writing until the inspiration you are receiving in this moment feels complete.

Journal

Let's journal! Grab your paper and pen. Take a deep breath and become aware of your thoughts and feelings. Bring awareness into your body, maybe place one hand on your heart, one on your belly, and take a deep breath in and out. With a sense of connection and compassion journal around these few questions:

1. What do you love about the form your Heart's Offering takes?
2. What is the starting point and end result for your audience from your offering?
3. How many people would you truly love your offering to serve?
4. What income does your Heart's Offering generate for your business?

5. Where would you love your Heart's Offering to be available and sold?
6. What does your biggest win for your Heart's Offering look like?
7. What does your product and pricing mix look like within two years?
8. What is the next action to take to bring your offering to life?

With your Heart's Offering emerging, bringing value to your audience, turning your true nature and purpose into a business, by creating it you welcome in connection, happiness, health and prosperity.

Your ego may love to barge in to tell you it's too good to be true, it won't work, who cares, nobody will want it anyway. The answer to this is to embrace your inner power and focus as your creative. Let's dive into that now.

CHAPTER 6

EMBRACE YOUR INNER POWER

"Our deepest fear is not that we are inadequate. Our deepest fear is that we are powerful beyond measure. It is our light, not our darkness that most frightens us."
-Marianne Williamson

Sitting on the gallery in Crabbe Hill Village, I gaze across the turquoise waters towards the Island of Montserrat. Monserrat is home to the Soufrière Hills Volcano, which was dormant for 300 years before erupting in 1997. Volcanic rock thrust with such force it travelled 33 miles to land on the gallery where I am sitting now. New deltas of land were formed, the town of Plymouth buried and people relocated.

This immense power within the earth terrifies and inspires me. Both destruction and creation spill forth, forming new landscapes.

We hold this creative power within us, too. No matter if this creative energy has lain dormant for decades. It can be ignited, rise up from within and bring forth new ways of being, give birth to new worlds and ideas. Invite it. Embrace it.

Your Focus Creates Your Reality

As you connect with your heart's wisdom, align with your true nature and purpose, your audience and offering, a whole wave of fresh creative emergence begins to spill forth, forming your True Business from deep within. It feels really good! You are energised, happy, making new connections, moving forwards with new possibilities.

Then in barges your ego.

"Who do you think you are? Are you crazy? How will you make money doing that? You will fail. You aren't ready. You aren't good enough. She/he/they do it so much better already. You will be rejected, ridiculed, humiliated. It's not safe. You will be taken out, maybe even killed. You aren't a business person. You are too busy anyway. Who will listen to you? It's too much hard work and you are already burnt out. You are always second best, so it won't work. No one wants what you have, anyway. No one cares what you have to say."

If you listen to this self-loathing dialogue, the wave of fresh creative emergence will be completely extinguished. It is like driving with the handbrake on or wading through thick treacle until finally you come to your senses and give up. You tell yourself, "The timing wasn't right." Or "It wasn't a good idea and wouldn't have worked, anyway."

You have a choice. To ride the wave of creative emergence or the wave of self-doubt and criticism. One is fun, energising and moving your forwards, the other painful, tormenting, abusive and keeps you stuck.

You can attempt to create your True Business with self-sabotaging limiting beliefs forged as a child; or by embracing your inner power and the deeper truth of who you are now as a wise, creative, well-resourced adult.

Notice for a moment, without any judgement, who is in the driving seat of your True Business? Your wounded inner child, or the wise, creative, resourced adult?

Embracing your inner power you naturally take new actions, form fresh new habits and behaviours that over time create a whole new business reality. You move beyond out-of-date patterns and behaviours into fresh new ground. You begin to embody the person you are becoming rather than the person you were in the past and with this transformation you also transform your business.

When I stepped up to begin sharing the wisdom from my heart in my True Business, I found myself gripped by fear, paralysed, unable to move forwards. A limiting belief "When I shine, I am shamed" was running the show. A few memorable childhood experiences had forged this belief.

At playschool, three years old, we were asked to sing a nursery rhyme. When it was my turn to sing, I innocently belted forth an off the cuff original: 'Cinderella went to the fair, golden yellow ribbons flowing from her hair.' And I was told off in front of the whole class: 'That's not a nursery rhyme, is it! Sing a proper one.' I felt ashamed.

At the 1977 Queen's Silver Jubilee Street Party, five years old now, I won the fancy dress competition. My grandma's friend had made me a wonderful Queen Elizabeth I costume. When I received the prize in front of the whole street, I was immediately told off by a neighbour: 'You don't deserve to win the competition! You didn't make your costume.' None of the children had. Again, I was shamed in the spotlight.

Like Pavlov's dog, these experiences conditioned me into believing that being in the spotlight was followed by shame. Fast forward into adulthood, a limiting belief now running unconsciously is that the spotlight is dangerous and best avoided. I'd never had a positive experience of the spotlight, so why would I want to step into it?

As a professional communicator, one of my strategies was to seek out male spokespeople I believed would be listened to and create opportunities for them to step into the spotlight and share positive messages and stories. I was in the background orchestrating, hiding and invisible, unconsciously avoiding any risk or possibilities of being shamed. Then I'd get upset when they received the credit, recognition and job offers in response to my energy and work! The wounded child was in the driving seat.

Launching the PR with Heart Online Course, I had to step up and become my own champion, the advocate for my own business. Embracing my inner power, a deeper truth emerged as, "when I shine, I inspire others to shine." This became my new focus and creative orientation for the launch, taking new action, growing into a new role as a visible, confident advocate of business led by the heart. Incredibly, the feedback from one of the participants at the end of the first course was: "Seeing you shining in your element has inspired me to shine in mine." By embracing my inner power, a new experience of being in the spotlight was created.

A former client was painfully wedded to a limiting belief: "Media can't be trusted." It was fascinating to observe how this produced such extremely different behaviours, actions and experiences to my own focus and orientation: "Media are my allies."

If media can't be trusted, you gather evidence to demonstrate this - there is plenty! You may recruit others who hold this belief to feel validated and right. When you meet a journalist you feel threatened, nervous and by being protective you come across as aloof and defensive. If a journalist is late to your launch event, you are upset: "See! They can't even turn up on time!" If articles don't come out as expected you deem media unreliable and conclude press isn't worth your time. You give up.

As media are my allies, I am curious when I meet a journalist, listening for their interests, values and where our alliance may meet. I've built deep and long-term relationships based on mutuality and respect that have spilled into friendships. If a journalist is late to a launch, I'm genuinely happy to see they've made it at all and welcome them and get them settled quickly so they can get the most out of it. If articles aren't published, I understand that happens and that the journalist is disappointed too.

This creative orientation has secured close to a billion dollars of media coverage globally across print, film, TV, radio and online sharing positive, inspiring messages and stories with a global audience. I've seen journalists moved to tears and wide eyed in wonder during interviews I've arranged and received emails with appreciation for being the source of their best stories and events.

A desire to grow your visibility and audience; to grow your financial success; to grow your business, to do creative happy work will require new behaviours, new habits. Limiting beliefs, doubts and fears, will rise to the surface for you to let go of and embrace your inner power, the deeper truth of who you are now, a well-resourced, creative adult.

The limiting belief "I'm not good enough to be paid well" was driving a client to give away services for free, under price or avoid their audience and projects all together. Letting that go, they embraced their inner power, "My wisdom and experience is valued and respected. As I focus on great service for my clients, I receive wonderful pay." This new creative orientation inspired new action, new behaviours and practices. They got their business off the ground in year one and doubled their income in year two.

As the leader of your own business, organisation or team, embracing your inner power, beyond the self-sabotage and unconscious ego agendas, is vital for your focus and ultimately determines the end result you create.

Acquire the self-awareness and knowing that you are a powerful creator and take responsibility for your focus and your reality. When stuck in an old pattern on repeat that is frustrating or harming you and others, identify the limiting belief driving it. Embrace and grow into your inner power and make this your creative orientation from which new action, behaviours and habits are formed and with it more connection, happiness, health and wealth unfold for all.

Shifting a Limiting Belief

One way to transcend a limiting belief and the pattern accompanying it is to embrace and communicate with the inner child who formed it. This restores a grounded connection with yourself and also holds the younger, hurt child within you that felt abandoned. This self-care practice repeated consistently develops inner awareness, resilience and strength.

Once aware of the underlying assumption running the show, close your eyes to go within and welcome in your future self who has this issue handled, bringing the well-resourced aspect of yourself to hold the enquiry.

Invite in your younger self who first experienced and made up the false limiting belief. Give your younger self a hug and tell them how happy you are to see them. Notice how old you are? Is there a particular sensation you are experiencing?

Ask your younger self how they are feeling? Listen for the response. Mirror back, I can see that you are feeling that way. Ask and mirror back a second and third time.

Ask your younger self what do they need? Listen for the response. Mirror back, I can see you need that. Ask and mirror back a second and third time. Meet any of the needs that you can.

Ask your younger self what do they most deeply desire? Listen for the response and mirror back, I can see you most deeply desire that. You can also say anything you'd love to your younger self and make any agreements, which you must keep to build trust and faith in yourself.

Repeat this self-compassion and power practice anytime you find yourself in a reaction, stuck in a pattern, emotionally triggered and overwhelmed. In doing so, interrupt the pattern of abandoning yourself and restore connection with your heart's wisdom, true nature and purpose. Watch yourself grow in emotional intelligence, confidence and ability to take skilful action and create a new reality.

New Power Centre Habits

A second way to transcend a limiting belief and the pattern accompanying it is to embrace your inner power and form new habits and behaviours from this creative orientation.

Taking new action you've never taken before may be a little uncomfortable initially, a little like when you first learnt to walk, until it becomes normal. Embracing your inner power makes taking new actions, forming new habits much easier.

Writing this book, I stumbled into a limiting belief: "You are insignificant and no-one cares what you have to say." Throughout my life, I have written for connection, healing, to make sense of situations and write 'things' into being. Suddenly, writing became painful. I'd numb out, fall asleep, binge watch Netflix. I'd join writing groups where they waxed lyrical about developing a 10 minute daily writing practice but I could no longer write! There was no way the book would ever be finished and then I was protected from the rejection of no one cares.

Embracing my inner power, a deeper truth emerged: "I am a writer who loves to receive divine inspiration and share it freely and generously so that it can go where it wants to go." Now I was eager to write every day! I didn't need to develop 10 minute writing habits because I wanted to show up every day to listen to what divine inspiration had to say and write. The limiting belief 'you are insignificant, no-one cares what you have to say' was robbing me of creative inspiration. Embracing my inner power as a writer sharing inspiration generously and freely new daily writing habits easily formed. I gave myself permission to write anything. Poems, articles, random journaling and explorations started setting me free. Creativity was healing me and my writing was inspired again. I was back in the creative stream, writing the next chapter of this book and my business into being.

Guided Meditation

Embrace your Inner Power

This three-part exercise will embrace your inner power as the creative orientation to bring about significant business transformation. This is often a huge turning point, a new perspective and direction.

Work with the key issue you are experiencing in your business now. Part 1 identifies and makes conscious the pattern and limiting belief driving this issue. Part 2 meets your younger self, who made up this limiting belief. As you listen and understand this past hurt begins to shift. Part 3 explores your heart's vision of what you'd love to create now in relation to this issue. This anchors you into your inner power to take fresh new action and create a fresh new outcome for you and your business.

Part 1: Identify the Limiting Belief

1. What is the key issue you are facing now in your business?

2. What are your thoughts about this issue?

3. What are your feelings about this issue?

4. How are you defining yourself, others and life in relation to this issue?

5. I am… Others are…. Life is….

6. How are you defining business, PR and Marketing? Business is…. PR and Marketing is…

7. What beliefs are you running?

8. What is the underlying assumption?

9. From what is this underlying assumption protecting you?

10. What behaviour and strategies do you adopt in response?

11. What reality does this create?

Part 2: Shift the Power with Compassion

With the limiting belief identified, you will meet with your younger self who formed this limiting belief. By listening to this abandoned aspect of yourself with loving kindness, you bring awareness and understanding and begin to shift the power.

Turn off distractions, close your eyes, and take a deep breath. Notice your thoughts and feelings. Bring your awareness to your body and relax your head, shoulders, torso, arms and hands, legs and feet. Where does this limiting belief live in your body? Your head, stomach, back, throat? Notice. Does it have a shape, texture or colour? Does it have something to say? What purpose does it serve?

Step into innocence, the bridge into your heart. Let your imagination take you into nature. Feel your feet on the earth here, your face in warm sunshine and breathe in the beauty and wonder. Hold out your hands and welcome in your future self who has this issue handled to place their hands in yours. Notice the energy and qualities of your future self. They have a message for you in relation to this issue. Listen.

Now welcome in your younger self, who made up this limiting belief. When they arrive, give them a hug, tell them how happy you are to see them, thank them for being here. How old are you? Are you facing a particular situation?

Ask your younger self, how are you feeling?
Listen and wait for them to tell you.
Mirror back: I can see you are feeling…
Ask again, how are you feeling? Listen.

Mirror back: I can see you are feeling…
One last time, how are you feeling? Listen.
Mirror back: I can see you are feeling…

Ask your younger self what do you need?
Listen and wait for them to tell you.
Mirror back: I can see you need…
Ask again, what else do you need? Listen.
Mirror back: I can see you need…
One last time, what else do you need? Listen.
Mirror back: I can see you need…
Make an agreement to meet any of the needs that you can.

Ask your younger self what do you most deeply desire?
Listen and wait for them to tell you.
Mirror back: I can see you most deeply desire…

Is there anything you would like to say to your younger self?

When you are complete, merge your younger, current and future self, back together as one. Open your eyes, come back and make any notes in your journal. Observe what is now beginning to shift and what is beginning to open up for you.

Part 3: Embrace your Inner Power

Let's turn to what your heart is called to create now in relation to this issue, as an adult from this fresh starting point. Be curious. Immersed in this vision, you will anchor into your inner power and craft a power statement, your new creative orientation from which to take action and form new habits.

You know by now to find a comfortable spot and turn off any distractions. Give yourself space and time to be with your heart's wisdom and divine inspiration, to listen deeply. When you are ready, gently close your eyes.

Take a deep breath into your belly, in and out. As you sit with the intention to embrace your inner power, notice your thoughts and feelings as a compassionate observer, no judgement.

Bring your awareness to your body, notice any sensations or tension. Relax your head, jaw, throat and neck. Drop your shoulders and re-lax your arms, hands, fingers. Now your torso, let your belly out, feel your sitting bones in contact with the chair, back supported. Relax your legs, feet and toes. Breathe in loving kindness from the soles of your feet up into the whole of your being. Send loving kindness to your audience; loving kindness to the Earth.

Step into innocence, the bridge into your heart, where you can listen to your wise inner compass and come into harmony with the fresh creative stream of Source universal energy emerging through you now.

In your imagination, take yourself back to your Essence Pool. Feel your feet on the lush green grass, warm gentle sunshine on your face and shoulders and as you take a deep breath in, your body relaxes even more. You can see and hear the waterfall making its way into your Essence Pool, down through the stream into the ocean. Breathe in the awe, beauty and magic of this sacred place, the humming of life here.

If you'd like to, you can stand under the waterfall feeling the water massaging your shoulders, cool silky water on your skin. The pure water clears your mind, washes away anything you no longer need in your energy field. What are you letting go of, what is leaving your system from this point onwards?

You make your way into the pool. Dive from the rocks, glide in from the bank or wade into the water from the shallows, just as you like. Fully immerse yourself into the water, into your true essence. Diving down deep, you can breathe easily under water and notice how this takes you into stillness.

As you return to the surface, recall your essence and purpose, "I am… Here to… So that…" and held by the water take a moment to rest.

After a little while you swim to the side of the pool to the natural rock formation steps that allow you to climb out easily onto the lush green grass, warm sunshine on your face and skin. You see water droplets on your body begin to evaporate in the sunshine and notice that you are relaxed, curious, open and deeply receptive.

On the Earth in front of you, draw a beautiful golden circle. This golden circle represents what your heart is called to create now as a powerful creator, a well-resourced adult, in relation to this issue.

Step in to the golden circle and receive your heart's vision, the essence and the full flourishing of what you are called to create now. Standing in your heart's vision fully realised receive the deeper truth of who you are, receive your inner power statement. Be with this for a moment.

What new habits do you form embracing your inner power? What obvious next skilful action do you take? What reality does this create? So it is, and so it shall be.

Will you create your business from an out-of-date limiting belief or your inner power? Take a moment to consciously choose and let that choice arrive into every single cell of your being.

When you are ready, take a deep breath and gently open your eyes, returning to the room. Pick up your pen and write until you feel complete. Add your power statement to your True Business plan as your fresh new creative orientation.

Journal

Take 20 minutes to become more deeply acquainted with creating your business from your power centre with these journaling prompts.

1. What do you create in your business by embracing your inner power?
2. What is more familiar to you - your limiting belief or inner power?
3. What becomes possible, fun, effortless as you embrace your inner power?
4. What shifts you from a limiting belief to your power centre?
5. How do you start and finish your business day embracing your inner power?

6. What new habits, behaviours and qualities do you develop?
7. What experiences have you already had of your inner power?
8. What skilful action will you take aligned with your inner power?

You have arrived at a fresh starting point, the creative orientation of your inner power, a new creative orientation from which to build your True Business. Fresh new actions, different behaviours, actions, habits emerge to accommodate the creative emergence moving through you now. Imagine 5 years, 10 years embracing your inner power to build your True Business. Where will you be?

CHAPTER 7

PROSPERITY

*'When I chased after money, I never had enough.
When I got my life on purpose and focused on giving
of myself and everything that arrived into my life,
then I was prosperous.'*
- Wayne Dyer

The turquoise waters at Darkwood Beach in Antigua are healing and magical. A small outcrop protects the beach a little so the water is often calm and clear. In the summer months it's heavenly. Wading into the cool, clear water with powder like white sand under your feet is perfection. This is where my heart spoke loud and clear during a 10 day holiday. "You are not done. You need to come back and float in this sea every day for a month."

So here I am. Five weeks later on a Tuesday afternoon, normally a work day. I'm immersed in glorious beauty, deep connection, peace and prosperity.

Only my mind is getting in the way. "What on earth do you think you are doing? Who do you think you are? Indulging yourself like this! Get over yourself. You aren't burnt out. Pull yourself together. Get back to work. Get some proper money coming in. Stop being so ridiculous. This is a work day!"

In this moment I had a choice. To let the mind chatter, guilt and shame rob me of prosperity; or to let a whole new experience of wealth and prosperity in.

What Do You Need To Be Prosperous?

Your True Business meets all of your needs for a healthy, happy, prosperous life. As you bring your True Business to life, share your heart's valuable offering with the audience you are here to serve, a new and upgraded financial structure emerges that meet your unique needs for prosperity. An upgraded relationship to money also emerges.

Profit is not the end goal of your True Business. Fulfilment of your purpose - being who you are and what you are here for - is. Money serves your purpose, full creative expression and contribution to a happier, healthier, prosperous planet and society.

What does prosperity look and feel like for you? Maybe it is connection to Source, inspiration, vitality and creativity. Giving your true nature, talents and gifts to the fulfilment of your purpose. Freedom to wander in natural beauty, to marvel in the miracle of the earth and oceans. A loving life partnership. Being part of community. Nutritious, chemical-free food on your table to enjoy with family and friends. Making a contribution to wider society and humanity. A peaceful mind and generous heart.

Traditional business with the constant pursuit of more – more growth, more profit too often runs over these needs. It rarely considers the physical, emotional, environmental and spiritual needs of a human being to prosper, for the earth to prosper. Hurting fellow human beings and destroying the earth's environment for growth and profit is brushed away as 'just business.' When you choose not to hurt people or the earth for money you are labelled 'not commercial' or 'privileged'.

Money may pour in to your traditional business but if you are overworked, burnt out and unhappy with your nervous system shot to pieces; if you have no time for loved ones or a loving life partnership; if your business practices are harming the environment, or other people how is that any profit at all? You may even be sacrificing your needs, be overworked, stressed and unhappy and not making enough money! Draw a line. No more.

As I followed my heart's wisdom, allowed my true nature and purpose to lead the creation of my True Business, I became aware of four non-negotiable needs vital for me to live a prosperous life. None had previously been met by traditional business. All four are continually met by my True Business emerging now. Connection to the divine outdoors in natural beauty; deep and real relationships with clients and partners; a community of visionary, courageous creatives who care enough to act; and freedom of creative expression.

As I work with clients to connect with their heart's vision for their True Business, they discover their own non-negotiable needs for prosperity and a unique business structure emerges to fulfil these needs with ease.

One holds a deep need for freedom of location and their True Business structure emerges online, location independent so they can travel between Bali and the UK. Another discovers a non-negotiable need to be with and play with their children when they come home from school, which is met by their home office and freelance contracts with flexible hours. Another discovers a need to be by the sea for peace and inspiration and their True Business emerges as a cottage renovation in a harbour village in Cornwall, UK for hosting writing retreats.

Listen to your heart and your True Business will deliver the perfect structure to meet your unique needs for a prosperous business, life and world.

Your Heart's Currency

Your heart's currency leaves you deeply fulfilled in a way that money never will. It is why you jump out of bed in the morning. You love to do this regardless of payment because it is as important to you as breathing. And in your True Business you are rewarded handsomely for it - financially, creatively, emotionally, spiritually.

Maxine Clancy, founder of Divorce Detox, shared with me that her heart's currency is restoring peace and harmony in relationships. She works with clients who are experiencing emotional trauma following a divorce, supporting them to take full responsibility and with it the power to create the healing necessary for healthy self-love to re-emerge. She is financially rewarded for her work, and it is restoring peace and harmony in the hearts of others that brings deep enrichment and prosperity.

My heart's currency is being a rainmaker of opportunities and miracles for my community and family to fulfil their visions and dreams. Clients create easily what they previously believed to be impossible and this makes my heart sing. I'm financially rewarded for facilitating this but it is seeing their eyes light up with the joy of a vision, dream and potential fulfilled that brings enrichment and prosperity.

What makes your heart sing? What makes you want to leap out of bed in the morning for more? Get to know your heart's currency intimately. This is your rocket fuel. It is the unique and life-changing value you bring to your audience and wider world. Value and respect it deeply. Give of it generously and lovingly.

Out with the Old and in with the New Money Stories

Your True Business upgrades your relationship with money dissolving any money limitations and out of date blocks and beliefs that have brought you to this point.

A lot has been written about money blocks and beliefs that retain you in a pattern. The Soul of Money by Lynne Twist is one highly recommended book on this topic. Lynne raised millions of dollars for The Hunger Project on a mission to end poverty and global hunger; and The Pachamama Alliance to empower indigenous people of the Amazon to preserve their land and culture. She has explored the human relationship with money deeply.

Lynne highlights three common limiting beliefs – money is scarce; there's an upper limit to the amount of money I can receive; and I am powerless to change. These key beliefs become mixed in with cultural conditioning, learnt behaviour and patterns passed on from parental and key figures to form a money story that you experience over and over again. That is, until your expansive heart's vision and vibration of your True Business moves and inspires you to upgrade your relationship with money; to make fresh choices that serve the creative emergence now.

"Money is evil. Money goes to everyone but me. I don't deserve money. I'm not good with money. We are poor people. Money knows best. Big money is vulgar. I can't hold on to money and will lose it! People with money are wasteful and entitled." These old scripts separate you from Source, stunt fresh creative emergence and hinder the full flourishing of your True Business and life.

Recognise old money stories, patterns and limiting beliefs, which may not belong to you. These scripts and stories are not who you are. Do not allow out-of-date money scripts, stories and patterns to hold you back, to cut you off from Source and opportunities.

Sitting with a billionaire for dinner, I took the chance to ask about our radically different financial situations. What had driven him to acquire a billion dollars? It isn't a drive I've ever had and I was curious.

He shared an experience at 12 years old when his parents were evicted from their home. The public shame he experienced at being forced out onto the street in front of all the neighbours was traumatic. He decided he would never be in that position ever again. This childhood trauma and shame were part of the driving force making up the acquisition of extreme wealth and financial security.

My childhood experience was very different. Mum grew up experiencing two family environments that came with two different financial backgrounds. Mum was born into a working-class, coal mining estate in Yorkshire in the North of England and when her mother remarried she moved to a middle class, detached home in Kent in the South of England.

The Northern working-class coal mining estate was a grassroots community that I experienced as full of down-to-earth love with people looking out for each other. Men working underground depended on each other for their lives. Families lived close together in small terraced houses. People popped next door to each other's homes, let themselves in and sat down for a chat. Food was often shared. I felt safe, content and happy here as a child.

The Southern middle-class environment was a detached house, tennis court, miles from anywhere. My mum tells us how dreadfully homesick she was at 13 years old for Yorkshire, for her gran, for her school and friends.

As a child experiencing these different financial environments I made up a story you can have love or money.

This was compounded by hundreds of thousands of pounds given out to mum's siblings in vastly different quantities under the false pretense that everyone was receiving the same. The inequity and lies created an uncomfortable undercurrent and a belief that "big money doesn't come to me, I wasn't worthy."

There were significant benefits to this money story too. I found ways to create magical experiences with love, grassroots community and connection that money simply cannot buy. I developed a natural capacity to make money and resources stretch further becoming a miracle worker with budgets, securing phenomenal results and returns on investments for clients.

This old money story is also not true! It is a script I had to shed to build my True Business where love AND money unite to serve a healthy, happy vision that benefits all and the earth. The personal growth, new skills, behaviour, habits, decisions required of me with this upgraded money story are ongoing learning.

Your True Business will invite, challenge and inspire you to evolve your relationship with money and transcend any old money scripts getting in the way of who you truly are and what you are here for. This is yet another gift from your wise creative heart for the benefit of all.

Did you know that a staggering 70 per cent of lottery winners lose all their winnings in five years or less. The same money beliefs, limitations and scripts lead to runaway spending, poor investments and the return to a conditioned money pattern and vibration. You will evolve and hold a new relationship with money through your True Business.

To become aware of, transcend out-of-date money stories and build the new relationship with money that serves you and your True Business to thrive now you are invited to return to Chapter 6 – Embrace Your Inner Power.

Explore the key financial issue you are facing right now with the Embrace Your Inner Power exercise. This will serve you to identify and let go of money, limiting beliefs and behaviour and open up to a fresh new experience of prosperity now.

Perhaps you are stuck at a plateau, money is scarce, you are feeling squeezed, powerless to change your financial situation. Perhaps money has dried up with cash flow issues, or comes in fits and starts with no consistent foundation, or you can't hold on to money when it comes in, money is not yet working for you.

Let this be the starting point to access and inspire a new relationship with money that frees you up to create the True Business structure that meets your unique needs for a truly prosperous life.

Your Jackpot Financial Intention

What is the monetary value of your Heart's Offering? What amount of money is your True Business delivering in your heart's vision? What amount of money leaves you relaxed, confident and free to fulfil your purpose? When would you like to receive this money by?

When the answers to these key financial questions are purely sourced from your heart's wisdom rather than ego-led agendas you form a clear financial intention to inspire a True Business structure that fulfils your prosperous business and life. So much so that it feels like hitting the jackpot!

This is an embodied financial intention, a clear and deep knowing with your nervous system humming in balance, even during challenging times. It is not a financial figure plucked randomly from mid-air, fantasy, wishful thinking or a figure rooted in a need to prove your significance, status, security or position of power.

Your heart is expansive, connected to the vision and value of your True Business. The amount revealed by your heart will be a far more enriching financial set point - whether a higher or lower figure - than any amount chosen by the egoic mind.

The structure to deliver a £200,000 financial intention may be different to the structure delivering £2 million, different again for a £20 million financial intention. Listen and follow your heart's expansive jackpot financial intention and the financial structure and opportunities that meet your needs for prosperity will emerge.

On the Antigua Retreat I recall a participant pulling out random figures for their financial intention from their thinking ego mind: "£120,000! No let's double it to £250,000! Double it again!" Connecting with their heart's wisdom £650,000 emerged as their jackpot financial intention with a very specific inspired product offering to deliver this, fulfil their purpose and meet their needs for prosperity.

A client running a family business with a turnover of US$1.5 million wanted to double their turnover, keeping costs the same. When they listened to their heart's wisdom, however, their heart began to sing and creative inspiration began to flow at US$7.5m. Out poured their heart's vision, offering and structure of a boutique eco-hotel, along with a range of products and services in harmony with the earth. This was a business inspired by the future rather than dictated by the past. The wealth potential of the vision highlighted the need for them to step away from day-to-day maintenance of the business and build their next prosperous chapter. They hired a business manager to look after the day-to-day running of the business.

There may be a number of steps towards your financial intention. If you have a financial intention of £240,000 per annum within three years, you may have a first step of £96,000 within 12 months; a second step of £120,000 within 18 months and so on. You may have an initial financial bridge to support you in your development of your True Business - a rental income, investments, a partner's income, part-time employment, a business loan.

Once you have connected with your heart's wisdom and sourced the deeper truth within write out your jackpot financial intention: I am lovingly receiving £$ (amount) for (purpose) from (source/ offering) by (date). For example:

> I am lovingly receiving $125k+ for a coastal stewardship education programme from grants, sponsorships and donations by 21 June 2023.

> I am calmly receiving £1.2m+ per year from the embodied leadership training business by June 2026.

> I am receiving £5 million+ a year serving global brands to reduce their carbon emissions by December 2030.

I am receiving £3,000 per month from rental income to support me to develop my True Business by December 2024.

Next you may need to take a breath and acclimatise your nervous system to meet your newly upgraded jackpot financial intention.

Catherine Hale, nervous system coach and educator teaches change-makers and heart-centred leaders and entrepreneurs to regulate their nervous system to receive more wealth without working harder.

Sit with the figure your heart revealed to you for your jackpot financial intention and notice the response from your nervous system. If your nervous system is activated Catherine recommends that you return to the financial figure that your nervous system can calmly hold. Then in your imagination practice slowly increasing the financial figure until you gradually normalise the amount.

As the jackpot financial intention becomes normalised, you believe and know it to be true, you can play and begin to receive inspiration for the structure that delivers this amount calmly, easily, in a relaxed way.

Take the pricing of your Heart's Offering and play with the number of sales required to meet your jackpot financial intention. They key is to play and in doing so you begin to free up inspirational clarity that devises a simple structure to bring your jackpot financial intention and abundance into being.

A note too that your Heart's Offering, purpose and being of service to your audience remain your focus. You are not chasing money, which only tips you into fear and greed and disconnects you from Source, universal energy and inspiration.

This dance between focusing on being of service to your audience with your offering AND steadily building a new financial structure that allows money to flow in easily may take a little time to develop and balance. Give yourself the space, time and patience to build the financial structure that will hold you and your business confidently, easily.

You may find adding a date to your financial intention brings up pressure, a fear of failure, a freeze unable to move forwards. Or it may bring a feeling that the date is so far in the future you don't have to take any action towards it yet! This reaction keeps you stuck in the same financial set point.

The invitation is to work with creative inspiration and emergence rather than your mind's current relationship with time and money. Your heart is wise and expansive and will open you to inspiration, fresh opportunities and a whole new financial structure and outcome that in this moment you cannot yet see. Listen to and follow your heart.

Guided Meditation

Your Jackpot Financial Intention

Now's the time to connect to your heart and receive the wisdom and creativity to create a financial intention that opens you up to prosperity for all. A sacred time to listen as you meet your Chief

Prosperity Officer. Be curious and let go of any preconceived ideas around your financial capacity, wealth and prosperity.

You may like to walk to clear your mind and take in some fresh air, move your body and energy with a dance or shake it out. Do what you need to listen with the love and devotion you deserve.

When you are ready, turn off any distractions and close your eyes. Take a deep breath in for four counts and out for four.

As we begin to explore a financial intention for your True Business that opens up abundance and prosperity, bring your awareness to your thoughts and feelings. Notice what's going on for you. Be the compassionate observer without any judgement. Simply notice your mind.

Now bring your awareness into your body. Notice any sensations, tension, clenching. Relax your head, jaw, throat and neck. Drop your shoulders, relax through your torso, let your belly out. Feel your sitting bones in contact with the chair rising up to hold you. Relax your legs, ankles feet and toes. Allow the sounds around you to bring you into the present moment.

Let your imagination take you to a country lane where you find yourself standing in front of a tall, black, wrought iron gate. It's a beautiful summer's day and there is a sense of curious anticipation in the air. Slightly ajar, you push the gate open and step onto the gravel driveway of a beautiful, old country manor house.

Walking up the driveway, you can hear the crunch of gravel under your feet and take in the sight of deep green lawns, a cedar tree, a fountain with dragonflies dancing in the water's mist, a sundial.

The scent of roses meets you from the walled rose garden bursting with blooms.

As you arrive at the door of the Manor House it's open, waiting for you and you step into the entrance hall with a sweeping staircase, artworks, tapestries on the walls.

Drawn to head upstairs, you run your fingers along the wooden banister admiring the artistry. You arrive at the top to find just one door into a room with light spilling through. This is a magnificent library with floor to ceiling windows looking over the garden, tall bookshelves with a sliding ladder to reach the very top. A window seat, map, drawers and a writing desk looking out over the garden.

Looking up at the books, they continue up and up as if continuing right through the ceiling, hundreds of thousands of books, each one representing a True Business, the full creative expression and contribution from a wise, creative heart.

With your palms open, ask for the book that represents your True Business. See it rise from a shelf and arrive gently into your hands. What is the cover, texture, colour, energy it transmits? What does this tell you about your True Business?

The pages of the book begin to flutter until they settle open at a page dedicated to your heart's expansive vision for the prosperity in your True Business. Perhaps words, pictures, sounds, feelings or colours emerge. Your heart's vision begins to spill off the page until you become completely immersed living and breathing your heart's vision and vibration of prosperity in your True Business.

What word describes this vibration? Notice the needs your True Business naturally fulfils for you to love being prosperous. What do you notice about your fresh new relationship with money serving your heart's vision? Drink this wisdom into every cell of your being, it is who you truly are and are becoming. You might even like to take a moment to capture it, writing it down, receiving more inspiration.

You feel in your element, at home in your heart's vision of prosperity. A door appears and you are invited to step through it, finding yourself back in the library and this time you are not alone.

Your attention is drawn to two chairs and sitting in one of them waiting for you is your Chief Prosperity Officer. Sit down and take a moment to become fully present with each other. Who are they? What qualities do they have in relation to prosperity that you admire? Perhaps they have a message for you in relation to prosperity?

You say hello and how glad you are to be with them.

Ask, what financial value does my Heart's Offering hold? What financial income does my True Business generate?

Listen and wait for them to tell you.

Ask, by when? By what date?

Listen again until they show or tell you.

Ask, what limiting belief and old money story you are letting go?

Listen.

Ask, what new skills and behaviours are you developing in your new relationship with money serving your heart's vision?

Listen.

What is the next inspired skilful action for you to take? As it becomes clear, choose to take this as an offering of love, no attachment to the outcome.

Listen.

Sit with your Chief Prosperity Officer a while, allowing the value and jackpot financial intention for your True Business to settle. Allow your nervous system to regulate to this new level of prosperity and possibility.

Thank your Chief Prosperity Officer and if you'd like to meet again, agree a date and time. Then, when you are ready, bid your goodbyes. Begin to arrive back into the room. Feel your feet on the floor. Move your fingers and toes. Gently open your eyes.

Make any notes. Journal about your financial intention that brings forth a structure that meets your needs for a happy, healthy, prosperous life, business and world.

Journal

Reach for your paper and pen. Here's your journaling questions to receive further inspiration and insight around prosperity in your True Business.

1. What does your heart's vision of prosperity in your True Business look like?

2. What are four non-negotiables you need to be prosperous and why?
3. Are you meeting these needs? If not, what changes are required?
4. What is the vibration of your heart's vision of prosperity in your True Business?
5. What is your new relationship with money in your heart's vision?
6. What does your jackpot financial intention open up and make possible?
7. What qualities and behaviours are you adopting in this new financial structure?
8. What is the next skilful action to bring your new financial structure to life?

Your jackpot financial intention revealed from your heart is set to open up the emergence of a True Business structure that meets your non-negotiable needs for prosperity – creative, emotional, financial and spiritual needs. Go all in with a 100% commitment.

Embracing your new money story and relationship will develop new habits, behaviours and actions to create this financial intention. This is a new financial reality you are bringing into being in a calm, grounded, relaxed way. You are responding to creative emergence, stepping into the Creative Flow with skilful action to bring your True Business to life.

CHAPTER 8

FLOW

"Those who flow as life flows know they need no other force."
- **Lao Tzu**

As I sit in Crabbe Hill Village in Antigua, writing under the raspberry tree, I stop and look out across the Caribbean Sea towards the Island of Monserrat, glistening in the sunlight. A cat saunters up the road in front of me. A lizard scurries up the side of the house. Butterflies dance about the scrub and a love bird coos in the distance. The trees are swaying in the breeze and a peace descends on the village. I'm struck by this moment of beauty teeming with life.

We can create in harmony with this natural flow of life, present to the moment. Here our creations delight, heal, nourish and even surprise us. We are pioneers sourcing and serving a fresh wave of vital life force, Creative Flow, which is always serving the highest flourishing for all.

Get in the Flow or Crash and Burn

Former elite karate athlete and now flow coach, Lisa MK Ling first experienced flow during a tournament. Two points down and 30 seconds to go she describes a deep and clear inner knowing that she was going to win. This was more than believing, more than trusting, rather she knew. She was in a flow state. After 30 seconds she had tied the match. She won the next point and with it the match. From this point on she made the study and attainment of flow her life's work.

Lisa describes flow as:

> "A state of being where you are completely balanced but not sleepy; completely alert and focused but not stressed. Your body is alert, your mind still, an almost meditative state. Time feels as if it slows down or stops. You love what you are doing and get your best results. Athletes call it being in the zone, business people call it synergy, parents call it magical moments."

I experience flow as an almost magical state with life creating through me. Fully present I am absorbed in the moment, transcendent. My inner and external worlds become one. People, opportunities, resources arrive as I need them. There is receptivity, grace and ease. A sense that life is serving the highest flourishing for all.

Then the ego mind muscles in with a barrage of critical comments and judgements. "You should have more money, more clients, more business, more x, y, z. You can't be trusted. You are a danger to yourself. You are a failure. You aren't good enough. You'll never do it. You always give up. You haven't got what it takes. You are too old. You are stuck where you are and it will never be any different. No one cares what you have to say. You have nothing to contribute."

If you allow this egoic mind to judge and dominate you separate from the flow. You are vulnerable to distraction behaviours to alleviate the discomfort of disconnection. Binging Netflix, drinking alcohol, eating junk food, vaping, smoking, medicating, shopping, anything for a dopamine hit and a moment of relief.

Decisions and actions made here take you down the same dead end road. You waste resources – time, money and energy. You push, force and try to make it happen. Ultimately, you deplete your life force and burn out. You may experience depression, anxiety, stress, disrupted sleep, inflammation, disease.

World and Olympic sprint champion, Usain Bolt shared in the film 'Sprinter':

"You have to get in the flow of life or crash and burn."

You don't have to be stressed and sacrifice your wellbeing to get results. In flow you realise your best results AND feel the best you can too. You are in harmony with the forces of nature, the power that creates worlds.

Following your heart to a thriving business that is in harmony with your true nature, the earth and universal flow will most likely challenge you. Uncertainty, not knowing how it will turn out or whether you will succeed or fail can be uncomfortable and this can ignite the running judging commentary of the egoic mind.

Accept this. Recognise it as resistance, a normal part of life and creating. Be compassionate with yourself. Take a moment to acknowledge your feelings and needs rather than pushing through. Reconnect with your heart with one of the many of ways introduced in Chapter 2 – nature, breath, meditation, dance, appreciation, prayer. Return to and listen to your heart's wisdom, intuitive guidance.

US author, Michael Singer in his book 'The Surrender Experiment' gives countless examples of times his egoic mind wanted to take him one way. Instead he chose to stop, listen and surrender to the flow of life's perfection. With this practice he built a billion dollar business and a spiritual centre welcoming people from all over the world. It is well worth the read to embed this practice of letting go and letting flow in your business and life.

During the coronavirus pandemic the travel dependent retreat arm of my business fell away. I hit the menopause and with it a foggy brain, low energy and a mild depression descended. A heatwave brought record temperatures to the UK, rivers dried up, fires took hold across Europe and a wave of grief for the environmental changes we could have avoided if only we'd listened to nature and changed our behaviour spilled through me. Tectonic plates were shifting beneath me and it felt as if my previously prosperous True Business I'd thought was set up for life was going down the plughole.

To begin with I struggled against this inner and outer shift. I fought to keep my head above water, pushed to make business happen. Frightened, vulnerable, panicking about the survival of my financial income I wasted money, time and energy on a business coach pushing in the wrong direction.

As I accepted this post pandemic, menopause falling away I surrendered. I stopped, and in the quiet, in the rest, I began to sense my heart slowly calling me to let go, calling me towards the birth of a new vision, new vitality, new lifeforce emerging.

We can fight and resist these moments or we can accept and surrender. This takes courage and a deep trust. A knowing that life's flow is taking you to the highest flourishing for all, life has your back.

We fight and resist when we deny, manipulate and try to force life in a particular direction. We strive, over work, over achieve to prove our worth, reach security, driven by fear, guilt and shame. We grasp, grab and chase money. We disconnect, veer from the path of our heart, deplete our life force and overload our nervous system. We block the flow and crash and burn.

Where are you pushing in your business? Stop. Deeply accept the situation. Surrender to the natural cycles and rhythms of business, life and nature. This creates an opening, a space for life to lead and show you the way. A space where you can listen to your heart's wisdom and gently open up to new possibilities.

Our egoic minds, society, conditioning want fast solutions, now, impatient, make your mark, get it done. My heart's wisdom recommended a summer sabbatical. Take a break, rest and reset. Off I went to the UK for time with family and friends.

Visiting my sister's beautiful orchard on a summer's day underneath a blue sky and 200 apple trees, I received the inspiration to re-record my PR with Heart online course to grow your audience and impact as a self-study programme. I was to run my own business through it at the same time.

Relaxing in nature, breathing, listening to my heart's wisdom I began to realign with my essence and purpose, audience, message, channel and power. I opened to a surprising yet obvious deeper calling to the ocean. A strong desire to work more with nature. A vision of collaborating with water; collaborating with ocean leaders taking solution focused action towards clean, healthy, abundant oceans, rivers and seas in our lifetime.

This vision makes me feel alive, it makes my heart sing. I can feel fresh creative inspiration and energy flowing from and towards this vision, guiding me on. Now it's up to me to meet the Creative Flow and ride the wave with skilful action.

Skilful Action Invites Flow

Skilful action invites flow and eventually momentum to bring your True Business to life. If you don't take action, you won't create your True Business.

Skilful action begins with connection, listening and receiving your heart's vision and wisdom. You receive the next action to take, in harmony with Source, and take this action as an offering of love, without any attachment to a particular outcome. No pushing, controlling, manipulating, forcing the outcome according to ego agendas. The skilful action as an offering of love is the end result.

This is not how we are taught to achieve goals. We are taught to select a random goal and take action to make it happen. We do x to get y. When you do x and don't get y you may beat yourself up, tell yourself you have failed, play the victim game and blame it on others, the government, the financial outlook, colonialization. When you do x and do get y you may get a sense of achievement, triumph and victory, which can be addictive. This is the hamster treadmill.

Daily skilful action sourced from your heart's wisdom taken as an offering of love is Karma Yoga. This is skilful action as devotion, as a prayer, in union with creative consciousness. Skilful action, karma yoga brings a very different business to life than business built on action taken in reaction driven by ego agenda.

Drag your heals, avoid or delay taking skilful action, procrastinate out of uncertainty, fear of failure, rejection or success and you block the flow. Inspiration dries up. You become stagnant, stuck and convince yourself it wasn't the right time, you didn't want it anyway. You undermine trust in yourself and universal flow.

Take skilful action, no matter your thoughts and feelings, doubts and fears and you move forwards on the pathway of your heart a little more. One, two, five, 10 years along the pathway of your heart you experience the Fibonacci spiral in action and creative momentum carries you.

Steph Magenta is a certified breath work facilitator, shamanic practitioner and founder of Integrative Breath based in Glastonbury, UK. Steph previously owned four juice bars and clean food restaurants, crashed and burnt out. When we first met, Steph was running women's workshops and looking after the marketing for a breathwork organisation.

As Steph connected with her heart, she received the vision of working with men. This was jarring and met with surprise and discomfort. She was comfortable, happy and safe working with women.

Steph could have dismissed and ignored this invitation for realignment and blocked the flow. Instead, she chose to listen and go with the flow. She took skilful action, offering up a men's circle. The response was positive and deeply healing for both the men participating and Steph.

Steph, dedicated to alignment with her true nature and purpose, continued to take skilful action inspired by her heart's vision opening up Creative Flow to bring her True Business into being. Her next skilful action to take was to complete working for others and set up her own breathwork company, Integrative Breath. She did it.

Steph established weekly breathwork online sessions freely available for anyone to try breathwork. Next came a 21-day breathwork Facebook challenge that attracted 1300 participants and breathwork facilitators from around the world offered breathwork experiences for free.

This Creative Flow invited by skilful action moved Steph to the centre of the breathwork field as an advocate, facilitator and trainer. Integrative Breath's first six-month breathwork training programme sold out with 25 participants. Steph's True Business was born and thriving.

Decision Making to Invite Flow

Flow requires us to become skilful decision makers. If you are stuck or stagnant, often it is because you are putting off an important decision and this stops the flow. Take a moment to listen and your heart, your wise inner compass, will show you the way, back to the flow.

When stuck making a decision, turn to this simple and quick exercise to connect with your heart's wisdom and explore the outcome of option A, option B and a third option C, the outcome your heart would love.

You may find option A or B matches option C, the path of your heart, or you may find your heart's wisdom opens up a whole new possibility and pathway you haven't yet considered.

A therapist client was stuck making a decision on the location of her therapy room. This was blocking the flow, taking up time and energy, and she was going round in circles. Should she stay in her therapy room with a commitment to hours and conditions she was finding challenging? Or should she move to a new more flexible therapy room? She couldn't decide and it was unclear why not. She was stuck.

She connected to her heart's wisdom and explored option A, staying at the current therapy room, which she experienced as harmful to her wellness, a clear no. Option B, moving to a new therapy room, was a little better but still not compelling. Option C, the path of her heart, revealed she wanted to be free from the obligation of a therapy room altogether! This is why she was finding it so challenging to make the decision. Neither option was in alignment with the path of her heart. She decided to listen and let both therapy rooms go.

As she followed her heart's wise inner compass, taking skilful action, the opportunity arose to return to university and complete her degree. There was no need for a therapy room at all. Her heart's wisdom was ahead of the game. Trust your heart's wisdom: it knows who you are becoming.

Guided Meditation

Creating with Flow

Let's step into universal flow with skilful action. Action as an offering of love and devotion to bring your True Business to life in harmony with universal flow.

Turn off distractions and find a quiet space to get comfortable. This is the moment for to you dive deep into your sacred heart's wisdom to show you the way.

When you are ready, gently close your eyes and take a deep breath. As you sit here in stillness, bring your awareness to your thoughts and feelings. No judgement, be the compassionate, curious observer. Notice what is going on for you.

Bring your awareness into your body and notice sensations, tension. Invite relaxation into your head, your jaw, neck and throat. Drop your shoulders and invite awareness, softening and relaxation down through your arms, hands, torso, let your belly out. Feel your sitting bones in contact with the chair, your back supported and relax down through your legs, feet and toes. Breathe in loving kindness up through the soles of your feet, legs, torso, arms and head, through your whole being.

Step into innocence, the bridge to your heart, to listen to its wisdom and what wants to be created through you now. Let your imagination take you to your Essence Pool. Feel your feet on the earth, warm sunshine on your face and gentle breeze on your skin. Take in the beauty of the waterfall, that makes its way into the pool, that makes way into the stream and out to the ocean. Notice you feel grounded, open, curious and deeply receptive as you take in the beauty, magic and majesty of life.

You may like to stand under the waterfall, let the water massage your shoulders and wash away anything you no longer need, clearing your mind and energy field. Let go.

Make your way into the Pool of your Essence – dive in, glide in from the side, or wade in through the shallows until you are fully immersed in the water. Dive down deep, you can breathe easily and freely underwater. Take a moment here to flood your essence into every cell of your being.

As you return to the surface, bring your true essence and purpose with you. I AM… HERE TO… SO THAT… Lie back held by the water and deep knowing this is who you truly are and what you are here for.

Swim to the edge of your Essence Pool, climb the natural steps formed in the rocks out onto the lush green grass. Choose to the receive the wisdom of your heart. Draw a beautiful golden circle on the earth in front of you, which represents your heart's vision for your True Business. Step into the golden circle, into the full flourishing of your heart's vision for your True Business.

Notice what is obvious. The sights, sounds and colours. Who are you being? What are you doing? Is there a word to describe the vibration? What is the inspiration being offered to you in this moment? Drink it in.

Step back into the clearing with your Essence Pool. You can see the golden circle of your heart's vision in front of you. Next to it, draw a golden circle that represents your current reality, where you are now in relation to your heart's vision of your True Business. Step into the golden circle and receive the current reality.

What do you notice? What is the limiting belief you are orientating around? What is this limiting belief protecting you from? What flow opens up for you and your business as this limiting belief falls away?

Step back into the clearing with the Essence Pool one last time. You can see both the golden circle of your heart's vision and current reality of your True Business. What do you notice about the contrast? This contrast is the gift of growth, creative vitality, lifeforce and transformation. Give appreciation for this expansion and evolution.

Return to standing in front of the golden circle of your heart's vision of True Business. Step back in this golden circle fully immersing in your heart's vision and vibration for your True Business. What do you notice? As you follow the flow, what is the next action for you to take as an offering of love?

Choose your heart's vision and skilful action to take. So it is and so it shall be. Relax and let the vision and the skilful action settle in. When you are ready, open your eyes and come back into the room.

Take the skilful action as an offering of love. Follow this universal flow and ride the wave of fresh creative emergence towards peace, prosperity and progress in your True Business.

Journal

Reach for your paper and pen and journal for 20 minutes of additional inspiration to the following questions:

1. What does creating your True Business in flow look and feel like for you?
2. What new experiences open up for you creating in flow?
3. Is anything blocking you creating in the flow? If so, what?
4. Who are you being in your vision of creating your True Business in flow?

5. What qualities, behaviours and habits are natural to you creating in flow?
6. What habits and behaviours have you let go of?
7. What outstanding decisions do you need to make to ignite the flow?
8. What is the next skilful action to take to follow the flow in your True Business?

Connecting to your heart's wisdom you have received alignment with your true nature and purpose, your audience, your Heart's offering, power and prosperity. This is your unique True Business blueprint. With this you have unleashed a wave of fresh creative emergence and inspiration. Riding this Creative Flow, creating your True Business in harmony with Source, universal energy makes a contribution and impact beyond your imagination; a lasting legacy. What would you love the legacy of your True Business to be?

CHAPTER 9

HONOUR YOUR LEGACY

"I was able to see that if I had a contribution I wanted to make, I must do it, despite what others said."
-Wangari Maathai, Environmentalist

In one generation, all the coconut palms from the village beach where I live in Antigua have been lost. Lost to disease, hurricanes and because everyone ate the coconuts. Coconuts fall to the earth, germinate and grow into new palm trees to continue the life of the coconut wharf. When all the coconuts are eaten, there are no seed pods to replenish the trees and the wharf dies.

I would love my legacy to be the village beach replenished with coconut palms, a fresh new thriving coconut wharf for the next generation to appreciate. And with it, the accompanying understanding and awareness to leave plenty of coconut seed pods to grow new palms so the coconut wharf continues for the generations that come after. We've cleaned eight truck-loads of trash from the beach, planted 25 palm trees, 10 coconut seed pods and will continue planting.

I would love this to be my legacy in business, too. Seeding a way of being in business that replenishes us, replenishes the earth, a win-win for all.

Legacy Inspires Skilful Action

What contribution is your soul here to make to the universe? By building your True Business you bring your soul's contribution and legacy into being. There's nothing additional you need to do, no additional legacy project, simply create your True Business and the contribution you are here for emerges.

Living your true nature and purpose, choosing to build your True Business in alignment and partnership with Source, universal creative intelligence, you make a contribution and net positive impact beyond any personal achievement, a contribution lasting beyond your lifetime.

Having a sense of your possible legacy wakes you up to the importance of showing up, being of service and taking skilful action. Awareness that your True Business can make a contribution and is working towards a purpose bigger than you can create a dedication that is focused and immediate. You brush aside laziness, self-sabotage and I'll do it tomorrow mentality.

As a young person, I was living out of alignment with my true nature and purpose in a world experience so far away from the values I held in my heart. This struggle created an eating disorder and poor mental health. The deep work, transformation, healing and love that arose from walking through this dark night of the soul that lasted nearly a decade is one of my, if not greatest, personal achievements.

One of the many strengths I bring from this experience is the awareness that you can turn situations around. It may take time, it may take deep inner work and commitment, but healing, restoration and transformation IS possible. This inspires me that we can turn business around. It may take time, but it is possible.

That the legacy of the True Business model could be to inspire new pathways of the heart in business that create connection, happiness, wellness for my clients, for society and the earth inspires me to show up every day. It inspires me to step beyond my ego where I wrestle with a shadow of inadequacy, to grow in the skills and strengths needed to write this book, share the vision and model generously and freely.

Writing this book, Tim Bergling, the Swedish DJ and musician Avicii, appeared in my imagination as the muse. Tim united and uplifted millions of people globally with his music. All the while, his creative, sensitive and generous soul was in conflict with traditional business practices focused on money making at all costs. 'Avicii: True Stories' documents these struggles and they are painful to watch.

A gruelling tour and promotion schedule of more than 250 shows a year fuelled a work addiction, drug and alcohol abuse, illness and burn out. When expressing an immediate and urgent need to stop, rather than being supported Tim was challenged and urged by his business and tour manager to continue and meet the tour obligations.

Tim died by suicide in April 2018. His legacy, his music, continues to unite millions globally. His death shone a light on the issues of mental health within the music industry, the cost of unhealthy business practices on the mental health and lives of our creative, sensitive, artists who live for so much more than money.

What would have been the outcome if Tim's creative spirit was revered, respected and honoured? What would have been the outcome if Tim's creative spirit was in the driving seat of the business as well as the music? This was an inspiration to me in the writing of this book.

My hope is that the legacy of True Business is to offer a way of being in business that is in harmony with our creative spirit, our life force and natural rhythms. To open up new pathways for the heart where our creativity and life force is listened to, honoured and deeply respected rather than sacrificed or destroyed in pursuit of money. Our creative spirit is our life force, vitality and wellness. It is everything.

Tim, as the creative muse for this book, inspired an urgency in me to share the True Business model as an alternative way of being in business that nourishes and supports creative leaders. To rise and lead the dawn of business serving humanity and the earth to thrive rather than the sole pursuit of profit. This potential legacy inspires me to connect to my heart's wisdom and take skilful action every day.

Your Legacy is Created by Love

Maya Angelou reminds us that our legacy is created by love, from our heart, and that it brings a substance to our lives far greater than any financial reward. Oprah Winfrey shared a conversation she had with Maya about a school she created in South Africa. Oprah shared:

> "When I had finished my school, and I was so proud of myself for building this school in South Africa, I went to Maya and I said, 'Maya, that's going to be my greatest legacy, this school.'

> "Maya said, 'You have no idea what your legacy will be. Your legacy is every life you've touched. Feel everything with love, because every moment you are building your legacy.'

In each moment, we can choose to lead with love, to lead with our heart's wisdom, and embrace our inner power, true nature and purpose, or with the manipulation of an ego-led agenda. A life lived with the absolute commitment to choose love and the wisdom of our heart is a legacy that inspires the greatness within us all.

Prepare for the Unexpected

World-renowned English natural historian and TV broadcaster, Sir David Attenborough has had the most extraordinary life exploring the natural world, planet Earth and educating us as to the beauty and wonder through the medium of film and television.

In the 50s David was commissioned by BBC TV to explore and beam the wonders of nature into our living rooms as the presenter of 'Zoo Quest'. In the 60s he became the controller of BBC Two but resigned in the 70s to focus on making pioneering television focused on the natural world. 'Life on Earth' travelled 1.5 million miles to 39 countries to document 650 species as an ambitious portrait of our living world.

David went on to make *Blue Planet I and II*, capturing ground-breaking underwater images sharing the wonders of the oceans.

Then in 2020, at 93 years old, Sir David Attenborough released *'A Life on our Planet: My witness statement and vision for our future'*, a legacy film. He highlights how he has borne witness to the destruction of half of the world's wilderness in his lifetime alone. At his birth in 1937, 66% of the world was wild. In 2020 only 35% remains wild. The ongoing destruction of our natural world is destabilising the climate and threatening human existence.

Can you imagine dedicating your life to exploring, recording and sharing the beauty and wonders of nature, to unexpectedly find yourself speaking out about its devastating destruction and loss?

> "When I began my career, I had no idea that I would be chronicling a story of change on such a planetary scale. One with such profound implications for all life on earth. We've brought ourselves to the very brink of a disaster, the likes of which we have never seen before. I've witnessed it with my own eyes."

In 'A Life on our Planet' Sir David Attenborough goes on to share what we need to do collectively as he offers up a manifesto to reverse destruction and create thriving. He has dedicated his life to speaking into being a vision for a future beyond his lifetime, a future he will not himself experience, a legacy.

> "We know what we need to do. To restore stability to the planet, we must restore its biodiversity. It is the only way out of this crisis. By making the right choices in the next 10 years, we can begin to re-wild the world and create a rich, thriving, sustainable future for ourselves on earth."

As a wise, respected and much-loved elder and an experienced and brilliant communicator and broadcaster, Sir David Attenborough is perfectly positioned to speak to global leaders and decision makers as well as millions of people through their television sets with this critical message and vision for human thriving. Whether we choose to listen and take skilful action is up to us. He has done his part. He has followed the true path of his heart.

When we follow the path of our heart, we often don't know what contribution we are here to make until we look back and can join up the dots. We show up, go step by step, guided by our heart's wise inner compass. Eventually the dots join up.

A Helping of Courage

An awareness of a legacy, a purpose and life of meaning bigger than ourselves gives us courage to follow through challenges and continue through the darkest of times. An awareness of a legacy, a purpose gives us courage to speak to the vision and transformation and not shrink back.

Born in Afghanistan, Khalida Popal, former captain of the Afghanistan women's national football team, loved playing football with her brothers growing up. When she became a teenage girl, intimidation from men and boys in her neighbourhood began. 'Stay at home,' they told her. 'Your place is in the kitchen,' they yelled, throwing stones and garbage at her.

Supported by her mother, also her school sports teacher, Khalida had the courage to set up a girl's football team and invited other schools to do the same. She actively encouraged other girls to play football and went on to become the captain of the women's Afghanistan national team. She became the first woman on the board of the Afghanistan Football Federation, campaigning nationally for women and girls to play football.

As her visibility as the captain grew, so did the death threats. Khalida was forced to flee to a refugee camp in India. Conditions were dangerous and she'd wake from nightmares of men with guns trying to kill her. Khalida's mental health deteriorated and she was diagnosed with clinical depression.

Her sponsor, sportswear company Hummel, helped her to safety in Denmark followed later by her family who were also receiving death threats. Denmark became her safe haven and her home where she set up 'Girl Power', a programme for women and girl refugees in Denmark to play football. Khalida is clear her purpose is beyond her, beyond football even.

"My purpose is bigger than myself, bigger than football. Football is a tool to stand for my rights as a woman and for the rights of my sisters in my country. No matter where in the world I am, I can still stand up and support women. I can use the power of my voice. This is my purpose to help as many women as I can."

When women from the Afghanistan national team started dropping out Khalida discovered the president of the Afghanistan Football Association, Keramuddin Karim, was sexually assaulting players in a hidden room behind his office. Khalida drew on her purpose and once again had the courage to take a stand for women. With support she opened a case with the FIFA ethics committee to investigate allegations from five players accusing Karim of sexual abuse.

Karim was banned from all sports for life, fined 1million Swiss Francs by FIFA for sexually abusing players and players affected received support and protection.

I remember asking Khalida, after all of this, what's next for you after all that? Neither of us anticipated there was yet another huge act of courage required of her around the corner.

In 2020 it was agreed that western troops would depart Afghanistan returning the nation to Taliban rule. The last date for evacuation was 31 August 2021. It was no longer safe for any women who had participated in the women's football programme to remain in Afghanistan. Many people were scrambling to leave Afghanistan and Khalida began a fast and unnerving process with a core team to airlift the women's Afghan football team to Australia and the youth team to Britain via Pakistan.

Khalida is creating a legacy of safe spaces for women and girls to play sports, a legacy of women's rights. She is standing up with courage to a belief system that suppresses and harms women and girls, taking practical action to birth a new reality of human rights for all. Her practical courage inspires me beyond words.

I share these legacy stories to inspire us all. There are always times when we feel as if we are failing, we can't go on. Take a moment. Choose to let go and allow your creative spirit to lead. Heed the call, develop and draw on your natural gifts and talent. Your legacy is right there in the DNA of your True Business. This is a contribution so far beyond any financial rewards, it is the lasting contribution of your heart and soul while a privileged visitor on this beautiful planet Earth.

Guided Meditation

Your 100 Year Legacy

Grab your notebook and pen. Remember to turn off any distractions and get comfortable. This is your sacred time to connect to pure Source inspiration and receive profound guidance from your heart that can transform your business and life. Create the space and time to listen with the care and attention you deserve.

When you are ready, gently close your eyes. Take a deep breath in, and out. Notice your thoughts and feelings. Bring your awareness to your body, noticing sensations, tension, clenching. Relax your head, jaw, throat and neck, drop your shoulders, let your belly out.

Notice yourself slowing right down. Take a moment to choose to receive your heart's wisdom, your legacy, and serve it with love and truth.

Let your imagination take you back to the beautiful Pool of your Essence, with the waterfall and stream that makes its way out into the ocean. Feel your feet on the lush green grass and take in the magnificent humming of life all around you. Take a moment to breathe in the beauty and stillness found here.

Go to the Essence Pool and wade in, fully immersing yourself into the water, into your Essence, your I AM…. And recall your purpose, you're HERE TO…. Lie back for a moment held by your true essence and purpose, confident in normalising the knowing of who you are and what you are here for.

After a while, swim to the edge of the pool and climb out by the natural rock steps back onto the lush green grass. Taking a moment to choose to receive the wisdom and guidance of your heart. On the earth in front of you draw a golden circle and this represents your 100 year legacy of your True Business. Step in.

Receive the full flourishing of your heart's vision of your 100 year legacy from your True Business. What is your soul's contribution to your audience, to the world? What does your legacy make possible or transform? What aspect of your legacy makes your heart sing? What is one obvious skilful action to take?

Choose your heart's vision of your 100 year legacy and skilful action to take. So it is and so it shall be. When you are ready, gently return and write anything you'd like to capture the inspiration until you feel the inspiration is complete.

Journal

Make yourself a cup of tea and take out your notebook and pen. Gently close your eyes and take a slow, deep breath in and out. Step into the vision and emotion of your 100 year legacy fully realised. Imagine the contribution from your True Business, your life's best work, is now a living, breathing reality. Journal for approximately 20 minutes around these questions:

1.   What does your 100 year legacy realised look and feel like?
2.   What qualities and skills have you developed to fulfil your legacy?
3.   How does your legacy impact your audience?
4.   How does your legacy impact the wider world?
5.   What does your legacy awaken in you?
6.   What commitment are you now ready to make in your True Business?
7.   What is the next obvious action for you to take in your True Business?
8.   What pathway is opening up for you that didn't exist before?

As you sense the legacy and lasting contribution from your True Business, allow it to inspire you into daily skilful action to make it a reality.

Allow your 100 year legacy to bring about a fierce strength of focus, courage and dedication to your True Business, knowing that this substantial contribution will bring fulfilment far greater than the plentiful financial rewards. This contribution will fuel you through any challenges you may face along the creative path of your heart.

For to live the full creative expression of your true nature and purpose, in peace on earth, is the greatest gift and joy you can receive. It is the greatest gift you can give to loved ones and the wider world. My hope is that we all have the freedom, privilege and opportunity to meet each other here.

All that is left to do now is to commit to your heart's vision, to your purpose, legacy and contribution of your True Business 100 per cent. We have one precious lifetime on this magical, wildly beautiful earth. Go all in. Be alive to all the peace, possibilities and beauty of life right there for us all every day.

All you need to do is relax.

Allow your heart to light and lead the way.

This is your Creative, Happy, Work. This is your True Business.

Your True Business Plan

Intention

Essence

Purpose

Audience

Message

Channel

Offering

Power Statement

Jackpot Financial Intention

Legacy

Glossary of Terms

Source – The Universal Energy, Creative Consciousness that delights in creating the moon, the stars, the oceans, the trees, the animals, you and me. You may prefer to use the words Creative, Divine, Creator, Energy. This is our life force and creative intelligence.

Heart – The sacred core of your being that holds your pure potential, true nature and purpose and is connected to all of life. When you listen to your Heart, you unlock your inner wisdom, intuition and creative power, you bring your higher nature into business.

Intention – The end result your heart is focused on bringing into business in your True Business.

Essence – Your inner being, your true nature, the energy you emanate in a natural, relaxed state of being and how people experience you. This essence of you is what you will communicate and share through your business for authenticity and impact.

Purpose - Your reason for being, direction, North Star, why you are here. Your purpose informs what you are called to create and contribute in your business.

Audience – The people your true nature and purpose effortlessly serve to thrive. You may also have other stakeholders you want to communicate with e.g. media, investors, government, community groups, donors, partners.

Message - The one thing you want to say to your audience and that you also most need to hear. It inspires you and your audience into possibility, thriving, fulfilment of your purpose and vision.

Channel - The optimal place you show up to communicate regularly and consistently with your audience, to add value and build authentic relationships.

Heart's Offering – Your signature product or service that provides the highest value and impact to your audience, fulfils your purpose and creates a financial return. It is a unique and distinct blend of your heart's wisdom, true nature and purpose, talents and gifts, life experience, training and development.

Prosperity - All your needs - emotional, mental, physical, spiritual, creative, environmental and financial - met naturally, without struggle or anxiety.

Jackpot Financial Intention - The financial intention that opens up inspiration and Creative Flow towards a structure that meets and fulfils your needs for prosperity – creative, financial, emotional, spiritual.

Flow – You are in harmony with your true nature, with Source, universal energy and the earth. No longer fighting against your true nature, universal flow and nature opportunities, people, resources, arise in divine timing, life is creating through you.

Legacy – The lasting contribution and impact beyond personal achievement that continues beyond your involvement and lifetime.

True Business Listing

Here's where to find more about the people and organisations featured.

Ray Anderson
Interface
interface.com

Maya Angelou
mayaangelou.com

David Attenborough
A Life on our Planet
attenboroughfilm.com

Lynne Beattie
Mrs MummyPenny
mrsmummypenny.co.uk

Tim Bergling
Avicii
timberglingfoundation.org

Julia Cameron
The Artist's Way
juliacameronlive.com

Maxine Clancy
Divorce Detox
maxineclancy.com

Maddy Cooper
Flourish
Flourish.world

Claire Dubois
Tree Sisters
treesisters.org

Craig Foster
My Octopus Teacher
seachangeproject.com

Simon Haas
Yoga and Dark Night of the Soul
simonhaas.com

Catherine Hale
Nervous System Coach and Educator
catherinehale.co.uk

Paul Hawken
Environmentalist
paulhawken.com

Wim Hof
The Ice Man
wimhofmethod.com

Homeless World Cup
homelessworldcup.org

Charles Hoskinson
Cardano
iohk.io

Nina Hossain
Bliss Organics
blissorganics.nl

Lisa MK Ling
Flow Coach
udflow.com

Steph Magenta
Integrative Breath
stephmagenta.com

Charlotta Martinus
The Teen Yoga Foundation
TeenYoga.com

Marie McAneney
Women's Intuition Mentor
mariemcaneney.com.au

Madalaine Monro
The Gentle Alchemist
madalainemunro.com

Khalida Popal
Girl Power
Girlpower.org

Suzie Poyser
linkedin.com/in/suzie-
poyser-a294a436

Katie Sarra
Institute of Relational
Harmony Studies
Katiesarra.com

Bex Schindler
The Mindful Kitchen
the-mindful-kitchen.co.uk

Tosha Silver
It's Not Your Money
toshasilver.com

Michael Singer
The Surrender Experiment
untetheredsoul.com

Tanya Smith
Leadership Consultant
tanyasmithintl.com

Lynn Twist
Soul of Money Institute
soulofmoney.org

Joe Wicks
The Body Coach
thebodycoach.com

Reese Witherspoon
Hello Sunshine
hello-sunshine.com

Katherine Woodward Thomas
Calling in "The One"
katherinewoodwardthomas.com

Creative Happy Work Meditations

The Creative Happy Work Guided Meditations included in this book are available for download. Let Kat guide you deep into your heart's wisdom to receive inspirational clarity for your True Business. Guided Meditations include:

Introduction
Your Heart's Vision of your True Business
Discover your True Essence and Purpose
Welcome in your Audience
Design your Heart's Offering
Embrace your Inner Power
Your Jackpot Financial Intention
Creating with Flow
Your 100 Year Legacy

Bonus: Business Decision Making with Heart

RRP £19.99

**Creative Happy Work Meditations |
Kat Byles**

www.katbyles.com

What's Next?

If you are called to work together to create or communicate your True Business either one to one, in a small group, or on The Antigua Retreat reach out to me.

If you would like to add the PR with Heart Course to your teacher training program to provide a bridge for your students into a thriving business let's connect.

I LOVE hearing the inspiration emerging from your heart and flowing through your True Business. Reach out and share your experiences, the insight and clarity you receive from this book, from playing with Source to create your True Business.

kat@katbyles.com
katbyles.com

Acknowledgements

Thank you to the Caribbean Sea and the pure Source inspiration that flows so freely in Antigua and Barbuda leaving me happy, connected, well. I am incredibly grateful to swim daily in these waters and receive all the inspiration for the development of the True Business model and writing of this book.

Thank you to the creative and courageous pioneers who fully embraced the True Business model, especially those of you happy to include your brave and creative experiences in this book. Thank you for bringing your heart's wisdom into business, for choosing harmony with your true nature, our beautiful earth and universal energy. Seeing your win-win creative contributions emerge is a wonder and delight. Seeing that a new way of being in business is not only possible but happier and healthier for all fills me with hope.

To the business leaders kind enough to be interviewed and share your stories of following your heart in business for this book and True Business podcast. Thank you.

Andrea Adler for editing the first three chapters way back when and your encouraging words: "This book can help many people. I'm eager to read the next chapter." Lucy McCarraher for being on a mission to get more women writing business books and bringing a group of women together to write, a place to complete the first draft. Rebecca Megson-Smith for a skilful edit that inspired a far better second. Thank you, I appreciate you.

First readers Rowena Roberts, Deb Lace-Kelly, Anne K Scott, Janet Aldridge and Julia Schneider brave enough to give me feedback that inspired a re-write to include much more of my true essence and heart.

Suzy Walker for playing with the title with me. Lucy Cavendish for being a sounding board for the back cover copy. Lisa MK Ling for being a wonderful ally in the field of flow and writing the foreword. And for being brilliant women with heart.

My family for encouraging me and being people I love being with. Especially Dad, a fellow 'scribbler' and truth seeker asking after the book and how it's coming along. Mum for your nurturing true essence. Lizzie for your warrior love for young people's natural talents, gifts and creativity. Alfred and Lily for your bubbling creativity filling us all with love, fun and hope.

Trevor for inviting me to Antigua to write a book and teaching a burnt-out English woman trying to control each moment to go with the flow. Thank you for our loving friendship and life in nature once a vision held in my heart.

Author Biography

Kat has championed global brands and entrepreneurs pioneering positive social and environmental innovation for 30+ years including Homeless World Cup, Nike, Good Energy, Vodafone Foundation, UEFA, Desmond Tutu, Eric Cantona, Colin Farrell and Lewis Hamilton.

In early 2000 she was the founder of Authentic PR for businesses with a purpose, pioneering the purpose economy now worth over £100 billion in the UK alone; and was Acting Publisher of New Consumer, the UK's leading authentic and ethical lifestyle magazine.

As Global Communications Director for the Homeless World Cup, Kat was instrumental in growing the organisation from 20 to 70 nations, positively impacting 250,000 people in five years. She generated $25+ million in media coverage and was executive producer for *Kicking It narrated by Colin Farrell*, selected for the Sundance and Tribeca Film Festivals and sold to US Sports Channel ESPN. She also secured the feature film, *The Beautiful Game, starring Bill Nighy and Micheal Ward* with Blue Print Pictures made for Netflix 14 years later.

Then she burnt out. Following her heart to Antigua, the Caribbean Sea restored her wellness and began feeding her with inspiration for the radical, regenerative business model True Business. This has since inspired 300+ leaders, teachers and healers in 14 countries to thrive with a new vision for their business in harmony with their true nature, the earth and creative consciousness.

Kat lives in the UK and Antigua with her husband Trevor, their dog Scratch who adopted them as a puppy. You'll find her on the beach cleaning the coastlines, loving and appreciating the Caribbean Sea.

katbyles.com

Printed in Great Britain
by Amazon